LETTERS HOME

Leslie Griffiths

for Wendy al Roger

with warmest good wishes,

Smestre '95.

🌐

Foundery Press

Letters Home

©Leslie J Griffiths

Cover Design Steven Hall

ISBN 1 85852 047 9

Printed in England by Clays Ltd, St Ives plc

Preface

This has been a very pressurized year. It has given me all kinds of opportunities to meet people and assess the health of the nation. It has certainly been a great privilege and I'm deeply grateful to all those who have helped me carry out my responsibilities.

Before the year began, Brian Thornton asked me whether I'd be prepared to put pen to paper once a week as if to write home to one or another of the members of my family. This would, he thought, enable me to share experiences and encounters with a wider audience. I was glad to consider such an interesting proposal and the family even gladder to give their agreement. And what a joyful labour it has proved to be!

The President of the Conference is as near to being in a state of perpetual motion as can be imagined. This can be very taxing for some, I know. For me, I have to say, it's been invigorating. I've thoroughly enjoyed the countless rallies, services, studies, lectures and seminars in which I've taken part over the year. I knew clearly that there would be two major thrusts to my presidency. The first would be to be with my fellow-Methodists, to encourage and affirm them, to challenge and uplift them. I've done my best to do this. The second thrust would be to represent Methodists beyond the boundaries of the Methodist Church. It's in this area that I've tended to identify subjects for my 'letters home'.

These letters, together with the weekly articles I've written for the 'Methodist Recorder', have given me a welcome opportunity to reflect on some of the things that I've been exposed to. As well as being active, therefore, I've been able to be reflective. I've depended on modern technology to achieve this output. My weekly article was produced on my IBM portable word processor. The contents of this little publication were spoken into my compact dictaphone. My fantastic personal assistant Kath Booth did the rest.

I am most grateful to Brian Thornton and the Methodist Publishing House for showing such confidence in me for this project. Kath Booth's resilience and capability have proved to be phenomenal. My family's patience and persistent encouragement has been constant. Margaret's stamina, faith, love of Methodism and unstinting support have kept me going all through the year. If what follows seems impossibly opinionated then, dear reader, there's only me to blame. But I'd like to think that this publication will enable 'ordinary Methodists' to enter into the presidential experience and enjoy some of its fun, share some of its high moments, and marvel at the number of opportunities there are to spread the Good News and relate Christian thinking and presence to the world at large. That's the spirit in which I offer what now follows. I hope they give some pleasure to those who read on.

Leslie Griffiths
May 1995

THE RECIPIENTS

Margaret, my wife, who's been able to accompany me for most of the year and who has helped me bear the weight of those extra responsibilities which have come my way by finding more energy than usual for household and other tasks. She works as a radiotherapist at the Royal London Hospital in Whitechapel.

Ruth, our daughter. After Kingswood School, she went to Cardiff University where she's pursuing a degree in Modern Languages. She came with us to Haiti where her good French was soon put to the test.

2

Tim is our eldest boy. After the Leys School and a year at Goldsmith's College, he's now a relief manager for a major chain of retail shops and lives in Brixton.

Jon, our second son. After the Leys School and a year at Reading University, he's now an assistant manager for the same major chain of retail shops as his elder brother. He lives in Camberwell until he needs to get some washing done or some decent food inside him.

Kathleen Rhodes, my mother-in-law. She lives in Newcastle-under-Lyme and is a devoted member of the Methodist church there.

Kath Booth is my personal assistant, wife of Mark Booth who's been 'acting Superintendent' in my absence as President. Without her there would have been a very attenuated presidential programme this year.

Dear Margaret

I find hotels ghastly. I'm writing this from a room that's lavishly furnished and fitted with carpets wall to wall. Nice pictures hang on the walls. The colour television offers me entertainment and instruction via the channels I'm used to as well as a myriad that come mysteriously down what's called 'cable'. The bathroom is hygienic and full of more towels than I could use in a couple of years. In fact, I'd like to bundle them all up and send them to one of those places in the world where there is so much suffering at this time. What could a hospital in Rwanda do with a metric ton of pristine towelling, I wonder? The sumptuous comfort of this room is seductive. It traps me in a lonely cell, it separates me from everybody.

I quite see why they put us all in these places, of course. It's so that we can have access to each other to discuss the affairs of Conference. But I remain to be convinced that the gain completely offsets the loss.

I've attended a string of Conferences and, at all of them, I've stayed in digs. As I cast my mind back to Derby, Newcastle, Leicester and so on, the nicest memories (sometimes the only ones!) are those to do with the people who were my hosts. What raucous laughter we enjoyed! How wonderful to be treated like the prodigal son, with a fatted calf and a laden table all part of the deal! What friendships were forged and remain alive to this day! Oh yes, give me digs any day.

Nevertheless, from the loneliness of this opulent room, I write this pensive letter. A whole year of 'designation' is about to culminate in my induction as President of the Methodist Conference and successor to John Wesley. My kids are telling their friends that they are coming to Leeds for my coronation! Some wag has told me how a bishop, on the day of his enthronement, noticed that the programme had misprinted the key word so that it appeared 'enthornement'. And I received a card from a colleague which, whilst it wishes me well, contains sharp advice: 'Soar high,' it reads, 'but not too high - remember Icarus!' I'll do my best.

One of the strange things about staying in this hotel is finding myself stuck in the lift with bunches of Divisional and Connexional people whom I've always tried to take on one at a time. Much more intriguing is to find a whole string of them sitting (as if factory-bred) behind predictable tables, their faces attacking laden breakfast dishes full of food that can't be doing the Church any good. They're a lovely lot, though. And yet, just now and again, something undoubtedly happens to the chemistry of Church big-wigs when they come together *en masse*. Nice interesting people can suddenly turn into what used to be called 'minor synods'. Thankfully, however, the World Cup and Wimbledon are taking place so there are other things to talk about and other jokes to share than those that have an ecclesiastical ring to them.

I've just had a go at framing a loyal greeting to Her Majesty the Queen. Until this moment, Her Majesty and I have not been on intimate terms. But now I am about to sign an official document that will be faxed to her at Buckingham Palace. I am longing for her reply. 'Dear Les', it might read and she'll sign, 'Yours ever, Liz'. Some hope!

It's just fabulous to think that only hours now separate me from your arrival with the kids and the great gaggle of Griffiths' friends and comrades. I can picture you on the train with buckets full of sandwiches and huge plastic bottles of Coca Cola, munching and joking and laughing your way to Leeds. It makes this lonely hotel room all the emptier and the prospect of your coming all the more joyful.

It's strange to think that the next time I write I shall write as the President of the Conference. You will let me indulge my delusions of grandeur, won't you? Only for five minutes! But you will also prick my pride as often and as sharply as you always have done. I love you and miss you.

Dear Margaret

I wrote the last letter from my hotel room. This one is being composed in an entirely different room, in the Leeds Town Hall, that has been set aside for the President. I shall never forget this room for as long as I live. When the Representative Session of Conference began last Saturday, this was where I waited for 25 minutes until the Conference was ready to receive me as its President. It's a big, light room, rather bare. It's not the sort of room where I can think holy thoughts or feel surrounded by a heavenly host of witnesses. It has a functional feel about it. Apart from a coat hanger, a large table with six chairs around it, and two sofas, there's no furniture to speak of. Nor are there any pictures on the wall. The ceiling is over twenty feet high. So the whole room has a feel of a station waiting room. And that, of course, was precisely what it was for me last Saturday.

I could just dimly hear the singing of 'And are we yet alive', the hymn with which Conference always begins. The sound didn't come with sufficient clarity for me to want to join in. I knew that after that they'd be saying their prayers, welcoming the Lord Mayor of Leeds, and having a jolly old time. All this whilst I waited. In the next room, as large as mine, Christine Walters was waiting too. We were as nervous as kittens. Every minute seemed to be an age.

Then came the moment when the prison doors opened and we were led into the Conference Chamber. I shall never forget that moment, either. The Town Hall was packed. The serried ranks of visitors and VIP's crowded down the steeply tiered seats, spilling over on to the stage. The balcony heaved with people. And there was an atmosphere of intense expectation. I could have coped with all of that, but then my eyes rested on you and the kids. There you were, all four of you, sitting together close to where I was to be inducted. Not quite close enough to touch, but close enough for me to feel your presence. I just wanted to cry. I don't know how I didn't.

I did enjoy making my speech. The audience so wanted to support me. It was easy to know what intonations to give to my sentences, what pauses to allow before continuing, and how to pace my delivery. It was easy because the people were somehow telling me how to do it.

Then in a flash it was all over and I was led back to this room again. It's such a prosaic place compared with the Victorian baroque so dominant within the Conference Chamber itself. And now, every day, I spend a fair amount of time in this room. But the nicest memory of all that I shall take from this bare old chamber is the tea party I gave on Wednesday. Ron and Gwen Ashman are in the Conference. They are in their eighties. Ron oversaw my first efforts at preaching and, I'm quite sure, was responsible for rooting me in Methodism in my late teenage years. And there they are, right under my nose in the second row representing the Southampton District. I don't know how many grins and winks we've exchanged in the course of every single session. The two of them are the most faithful fan club anybody could ever wish to have. So I invited them to tea. You'd think I had given them tickets for all the rugby Internationals at Cardiff Arms Park until the Millenium! They came with a child-like pleasure and excitement that I shall never forget. 'Oh Les,' said Gwen, 'to think that we were with you from the beginning!' And, of course, they were. And they deserve more than a tea party. But such unalloyed happiness is so rare. I savoured and enjoyed it very much.

Well, the capacity of this stark room to inspire any further paragraphs from me has reached its limit. The Conference awaits. I must go and preside over yet another debate. But I have enjoyed this little time with you. God Bless and keep smiling.

Dear Margaret

I am writing this in a small room in a University Hall of Residence. I'm aware that the previous two letters I've sent were overpoweringly conscious of the rooms where they were being written. But, after the lonely hotel room and the spacious room in the Town Hall, this has a scale more in keeping with my own self-understanding. I sit here and write, conscious that only a week ago some undergraduate was whooping it up at the end of his/her university year. Little bits of Blu-Tack on the wall are a hint of the posters that adorned the room so recently. No doubt they were of pop-stars, art and (possibly) even members of family. But, without any doubt, they opened up the cramped dimensions of this room with cultural and associational horizons that were virtually limitless. Now, without them, it all feels tawdry and small.

I'm here for the General Assembly of the United Reformed Church which is meeting on the campus of Lancaster University. It does seem strange so soon after our own Conference to be present at another gathering of Christians in this way. But I'm delighted to be here. After all, I am the first Recognised and Regarded minister of the URC to be the President of the Methodist Conference. Somehow, however, I haven't much stomach for sitting through the debates. I've had enough of that for a year! The chance to meet representatives and church leaders, including a number of old friends, however, makes the trip eminently worthwhile.

I was asked to bring greetings to the Assembly. I did so with pleasure and, in the course of my remarks, told a story you've heard me tell more often than any other. The story, of course, of the first marriage I performed. Do you remember it? The Newmarket jockey, all four feet two inches of him, and his Amazonian bride who must have risen to five feet eleven? I know you've told me again and again that the first time you remember me telling this story the groom was four feet eleven and the bride five feet three! No doubt the telling of the tale becomes more effective by diminishing the one and aggrandising the other. But I shall never forget the exchange of question and answer that almost reduced me to blubber on the floor of the church in Cambridge where I was performing the marriage. 'Wilt thou take this woman to thy lawful wedded wife?' I asked. He, little man, gazing adoringly up towards the mountainous heights where his beloved was to be found, opened his mouth and said, so innocently, 'I wilt.' The Assembly laughed and so did I, for the memory continues to refresh me all these years later.

Back to this little room where I'm writing from. I think of our boys' attempts to go through the University system. I still remember with pain their decision to withdraw after a year each. And yet I can't but be sympathetic with their fears of not getting a job even when they were furnished with a University degree. And I remember the 'debt culture' into which they were sinking fast and the difficulty of getting interviews with their tutors in these days when staff/student ratios are so unfavourable to the struggling student, and the poor library facilities, and the seldom-meeting seminar and tutorial groups, and all those other ways in which their University education seemed so inferior to how it all was for me. But I also think of our beloved Ruth who has just successfully completed her first year in Cardiff and seems likely now to go through and complete her degree. Sitting here, thinking of the young man or woman who was here just a week ago, fills my heart and soul with regret about the changed nature of higher education in these days when it has at last ceased to be an elitist occupation. In my day 7.2% of the people aged 18-24 went to University. Now a full third of them go and I'm not sure, since the expansion hasn't been matched with the proportional increase in resources, that they get a fair deal.

Well, this is turning out to be heavy stuff. But tomorrow I'll 'let the train take the strain' and speed back to London and home. God Bless and see you soon.

Dear Kath

Just at the moment I seem to be caught up in a round of activities associated with the world of politics, and especially the politics of the left. In my Conference speech, I said how urgently we needed a change of Government. That, of course, has been heard as a partisan plea from a covert Labour Party supporter. People, or rather many people, have failed to hear the more constitutional point I was making, that to have a single party in Government for a period of 15 years is at odds with our political process. Anyway, that's all over now. But add to that my visit to Tolpuddle where I've been keeping pretty dubious company and the picture begins to form itself.

I was engaged in discussion with Sir Rhodes Boyson on the 'Sunday' programme where he seemed unready to allow me to compare present day industrial relations with those of the 1830's which produced the Tolpuddle Martyrs. Interestingly, he telephoned me the day after my visit to Dorset to tell me how much he'd enjoyed our mini debate over the air waves. I told him how I suspected that if he'd been alive in 1834 he would himself have been one of the Martyrs. 'Strangely enough,' he said, 'if I'd had a little extra time that's precisely what I would have said.' So great minds think alike! I've already had the first few letters of protest that suggest I've besmirched the integrity of my office by being seen in the company of trade unionists, secular bodies and a whole array of politically well-known faces like John Prescott, Jimmy Knapp and John Monks.

But of all this coincidental political activity, the one event which will stand out longest in my mind was the service in Westminster Abbey to commemorate John Smith, the recently deceased leader of the Labour Party. I was taking part in the service. My mind inevitably went back to those streets in Burry Port where I lived in my youth and all those simple and lovely people there whose horizons are pretty much the same now as they were then. What would we have thought if we'd supposed that one day I should be marching in procession with the Archbishop of Canterbury and the Canons of Westminster Abbey and leaders of other Churches for such a service as this? It was an awe-inspiring event. The Archbishop of Canterbury spoke about John Smith being 'everyman'. He praised his integrity and goodness. There were various choral items sung with that degree of perfection that is surely unique to English Church music. I shared in prayers with the Moderator of the Church of Scotland, the Roman Catholic Bishop of Southwark and the Moderator of the Free Church Federal Council (Kathleen Richardson). My prayer was for the Christian Socialist Movement and for all 'who encourage matters of debate in faith and social order'.

There were two very memorable aspects of the service. First of all, Mrs Smith and her three daughters all sitting facing me in their black dresses and with their sad faces. To have John Smith snatched from them so suddenly still struck me as bearing the marks of real tragedy. And secondly, for all the beauty of the Choir and the wonderful organ music made by the Abbey organist, nothing matched the simple ethereal music played by, of all things, the Grimethorpe Colliery Band.

Who would ever have imagined that this group of musicians, who learned their harmony as members of now-decimated coal mining communities, should be able to bring their music into the Gothic interior of such a historic place as the Abbey and win the hearts and the minds of every single person gathered there? I never saw the band physically. They told me afterwards that it was in some lofty and hidden place above the choir. But its music, made for heaven, gave precisely the right note for such an occasion. The finishing touch of this great event was the quotation of John Smith's that appeared near the front of the programme, his last words spoken at his vivacious best at a dinner the night before he died. 'The opportunity to serve our country: that is all we ask.' And he was denied it.

Well, there you are, such a privilege to be involved in this way. Where next I wonder?

Dear Kath

We've arrived safely in Foss. This is such a pretty place.
We got to Euston Station very early this morning, and delight of
delights, put our car in the hands of British Rail! We sat in
splendid first class comfort and were delivered to Glasgow well
fed and on time. The 85 mile drive here passed without incident.
The beauties of Loch Lomond were enchanting and now a week
in splendid isolation stretches out ahead of us. What a way to
celebrate our Silver Wedding! It's all the better for knowing that
this will be our last holiday until I lay down the mantle of my
Presidency.

I must tell you about last evening. We arrived back from
the Buckingham Palace Garden Party at about six-thirty. It had
been a strange afternoon. I was delighted that we were able to
go. But it was a strange event for all that. It reminded me of that
scene at Ascot in 'My Fair Lady'. All those posh and foppish
people who seem to get great delight out of parading themselves
around in clothes they wouldn't otherwise be seen dead in.
Impossibly delicate eats provided from an extraordinary canvas-
covered buffet. Two military bands playing merrily on; if you got
to the right part of the garden you could hear them both at the
same time. We walked round a lake and were so relieved to see
over the bottom of the back wall of the Palace gardens our own
beloved number 82 bus making its way in the real world outside.
It was curious to see the number of Bishops present. No wonder
they don't want to let go of the Establishment. But the Queen
seemed to be able to relate to all sorts and conditions of men and
women. I never cease to admire her despite all my negative
feelings about privilege and class and the rest of it.

We got home, as I said, about six-thirty. I got down
immediately to my 'Recorder' article. I wanted to record my
impressions of the garden party and needed to get it off my desk
before we left. I'd nearly finished when I received a call from the

BBC. Radio 4's Ten O'clock News were wanting to do a piece on Haiti. Could I come down to the studio? Whenever that question is asked I know that they want me there NOW! As it happened, I was near enough finishing my piece for the 'Recorder' for me to oblige. So I promised them I'd come.

I drove down the Finchley Road and through Regent's Park, parking my car outside Broadcasting House. I went to the fourth floor and met the man who was going to interview me. I could see at once that he was prevaricating. He didn't have the gut or the courage to tell me that they'd found more interesting people to interview than me. So he took me into a studio and we went through the motions of conducting an interview about the state of affairs then prevailing in Haiti. The United Nations were about to pass a resolution allowing for the possibility of a military intervention. I gave them their five minutes worth and got back to my car and drove home. Margaret told me that she'd received a call from the same office and was sure that they no longer wanted me to come. When I heard the programme later in the evening I wasn't surprised that they hadn't used any of my interview at all. After all, how can I compare with the comments of the United States Ambassador to the United Nations and the BBC foreign correspondent in the streets of Port au Prince itself? But I'm pretty fed up with the way the BBC treated me, for all that.

Before I set out for Broadcasting House, I got a call from the Foreign News Editor of the 'Observer' newspaper. Was there any way I could do a 'Commentary' for Sunday's paper? They were all upset about the dreadful things happening in Rwanda and were conscious that, while they'd treated it extensively at the level of news, they hadn't offered much analysis of the events there. They particularly wanted an ethical or moral comment upon genocide and how the international community ought to be treating instances of ethnic cleansing and the like. They wondered whether I could deliver 1100 or 1200 words by ten o'clock on Saturday morning. I told them I'd have a go.

I knew this was a new league for me. I knew equally that I'd have to get it absolutely right or they'd have to find someone else. But I had a go. Until two o'clock in the morning I worked hard at examining the whole issue of genocide. I looked at the need to establish a convention whereby those who perpetrate crime against humanity can be called to trial after the event. People who give the orders to perpetrate the kind of things that have been happening in Rwanda (and before that in Bosnia) need to know that they will not simply have their crimes overlooked when the media have taken their circus elsewhere. I finished the article at two o'clock and I faxed it to the 'Observer' before going to bed.

I was up at six to get ready for our journey here. I wasn't surprised when the Foreign News Editor rang me to say that they had debated long and hard whether to include my piece and had decided it wasn't quite what they wanted. At least with her, unlike the BBC, I knew on what basis we were negotiating. And she was very nice indeed. And I hope she might give me another opportunity later on. I've learned a great deal from wrestling to produce a piece that I thought was in line with the house style and the requirements of the editorial team of the 'Observer'.

So you see, my coming here has not been without incident. Last night was certainly not the evening I'd planned it to be. But I must say that I do enjoy working under pressure.

But now I'm under no pressure and I'm enjoying that just as much. All good wishes to you in the heat of London as Margaret and I bask in the cool and the loveliness of Scotland. See you soon.

28th July 1994

Dear Kath

This has been a wonderful interlude of peace and tranquillity amidst the pressing duties of this frenetic year. Scotland is not only brave, it's exceedingly beautiful. The glens, the lochs, the vistas are fantastic. We stood where Bonnie Prince Charlie raised his standard at Glen Finnan and relived in our inner minds the progress of the '45 rebellion'. And we stood at Culloden and saw that place of utter despair where thousands of Scottish fighters met their gruesome end. But we've also followed a different political career. We saw Glamis Castle and then Cawdor Castle and thought, of course, of Macbeth. After he got Glamis and Cawdor, he took the Scottish throne by murdering its rightful owner. All this history, the story of empty ambition and lofty ideals, of 'strutting and fretting our hour upon the stage' was laid out before us in the midst of the most exquisite scenery.

The beauty of Scotland was just one feature of our little holiday (and clothed almost perpetually in sunshine at that!). We also enjoyed magnificent fellowship with Ann and Arthur Valle. Arthur was Margaret's minister when she was a teenager and we've seen very little of each other since. But it was to their house in Foss that we went for our honeymoon 25 years ago and, naturally, thought how perfect it would be if we celebrated our Silver Wedding in the same place. This time, we not only had the house but we also had its owners! Far from being an inhibiting factor, this proved to be the most amicable and indeed blessed arrangement. Margaret and I were thoroughly spoiled by Scottish hospitality of the most lavish kind. Who said that Scots were mean?

And we explored Scottish culture together, reading poetry and dilating upon Scottish hopes and aspirations. We went twice to the theatre and ate wonderful meals at the Pitlochry Festival Theatre. What a marvellous time we had! I hope this doesn't

16

turn you green with envy in what our newspapers tell us is the hottest and muggiest July London has known since 1769 – the year that ice cream was invented.

No more for this time. Soon this moment of blessedness will come to its end and the gears will change.

12th August 1994

Dear Margaret

I'm in my hotel room in Lilongwe, the capital city of Malawi, at the end of my ten days in this beautiful country. I don't think I want to rehearse here the various things that have happened on this trip which I've reported in two articles in the 'Methodist Recorder' (11 and 18 August) which you will have read before this gets to you. The picture has been dominated by refugees, drought, AIDS, the sheer beauty of the country and the docility of its people.

A highlight was undoubtedly my contact with the Kandiero family. They'd been members of our church in Golders Green throughout our first three years there. It was wonderful to see Tony again after nine months back here. But seeing him brought back all those occasions when he was High Commissioner in London and I used to visit him through some very difficult times. He'd been appointed by the President of Malawi, Dr Hastings Banda. He was expected to behave impeccably as his master's voice in Britain. But there were key points at which he disagreed with his Government.

For example, he was forbidden to have contact with the recently un-banned ANC, a legacy of Banda's long-term links with apartheid South Africa. Even so, he defied that injunction and cultivated a good relationship with ANC leaders in London. Then, when the Roman Catholic Bishops published their pastoral letter in March 1992 demanding that human rights be honoured and free speech and association be encouraged, a bombshell that was to have an incredible effect on life in Malawi, Tony was expected to take a strong line of condemnation and make representations to Roman Catholic authorities in Europe. But he was, to say the least of it, ambivalent on the issue. There were spies in his High Commission staff who reported his every move back to Lilongwe.

Whenever I visited him, we had to go out into the garden when our conversation touched on sensitive issues, because he was convinced that his house was bugged. In the end, the Banda Government could no longer tolerate him. He was summoned home peremptorily and the rest of his family followed months later. But now, of course, he's been thoroughly vindicated and it was wonderful to see them all together in their Blantyre home.

Just before I left them for the last time, they fell into that way of talking that suggests that something of moment is about to happen. Sure enough, they announced that they wished to give me a present to take back to England. When they produced it, it turned out to be a chief's chair and the back of it stands five feet tall! I sat in it and they told me that I looked the part. And then they gave me the chair and now I have to manage as best I can to carry it from Malawi to Zimbabwe, from Zimbabwe to Mozambique, and from Mozambique to South Africa before returning to England. About seven planes and airlines will have to receive this enormous item that I shall carry round like the Ancient Mariner's albatross!

We've met many people in the time we've been here from all walks of life. On one evening last week we met the very interesting General Secretary of the Blantyre Synod of the Presbyterian Church, Dr Silas Ncosana. He was accompanied by Brian Kandiero, Tony's brother, who's a leading lay official in the Synod. And there was a third person there sitting at the end of the table with a large calculator in front of him. We were told he was the Synod Accountant and would be available in case there were financial calculations to be made. He never said a word. The extraordinary thing is that we were told his name was Macbeth! That's all, just Macbeth. I remember the scene in the play of that name where Macbeth, now king of Scotland, is haunted by the presence of Banquo's ghost (at a dinner he gives). Well, at our meeting we seemed very much haunted by a ghost called Macbeth. He was there the whole time but said absolutely nothing. Nor did he ever need to use his calculator.

Several times now, I've seen trucks full of white tourists. They've all been going on some trans-African expedition and their transport looks pretty uncomfortable. It seems that they find some field or a beach and spend the night there before continuing their trek the next morning. It's been most interesting getting the local people's view of these marauders hurtling through their countryside. It appears that they make no effort to get to know the people or the culture of the places they visit. They just keep rolling along. Today, on our way back to the capital city ready to leave Malawi we passed through a town with the extraordinary name of Nkhotakota. Whilst there, a Landrover pulled over to fill up with petrol at the little filling station where we were drinking a Coca Cola – that ubiquitous drink that seems to have got to the remotest corners of the earth.

The Landrover was full of young people who, as conversation proved, had driven from Kenya to Zimbabwe and now were on their way back to Kenya. They were all Oxford students. I spoke to a young lady who'd just taken her degree and got a first in theology. She had no idea what to do. She was going back to Britain scratching her head as to where her future lay. 'I'm not really a Christian,' she said. 'And I've no skills whatsoever.' She then started to ask me for my advice and we had a good conversation. But I ruminated about these clever kids seeing the world, without really having formed a view about its values and meaning. They often seem so aimless. Tomorrow I leave Malawi for Zimbabwe.

Dear Margaret

I'm writing this from a situation as different from some of my experiences in Malawi as could be possibly imagined. I'm staying with Richard and Elizabeth Dales. Richard is the British High Commissioner in Zimbabwe and an old friend of mine. I'm sitting in a suite of rooms made over to me for the three days I'm here. The house is simply palatial. It has its own swimming pool, tennis court and squash courts. It's surrounded by a perimeter fence that is constantly patrolled by uniformed security men.

Within the house there are reception rooms and outside a patio on which functions are held and visitors received. The walls of the house are adorned with pictures from the National Archive, and some are very splendid and historical. As I signed the visitors' book I noticed a few entries before mine the signature of the Princess of Wales, and a large number of Government ministers. It's all very grand and I'm enjoying it all. Viscount Tonypandy (George Thomas) once said to me: 'I'm against privilege, but I love it!'

In my weekend here I've had a variety of experiences that have been most interesting. With the Dales, I spent 36 hours on the farm of a very wealthy Zimbabwean about 70 or 80 miles from the capital city. He has five thousand acres and cultivates corn and tobacco. He has 250 head of cattle and breeds race horses. He's beginning to develop citrus groves and is himself building an enormous dam so that he can control the water supply to the various parts of his estate.

Once again, as in so many places here, you cannot but be aware of security. The whole estate is surrounded by a fence and an armed guard is constantly kept on its perimeter. Zimbabwe, like Malawi, is awash with cheap and easily available weapons, the leftovers (as it were) of the wars in neighbouring states and indeed the struggle in this country itself. But the farm where we were borders what is called 'communal land' where black Zimbabweans eke out their much more meagre existence. The farmer we were with is extremely good in his relationships with these people. But the rich farm owned by the white farmer stands as a comment on the curious way in which title to land seems to be held by white people and 'communal' ownership (without title) rests with the blacks.

With the farmers and the Dales I went to church yesterday morning. What a curious experience that was! It was an Anglican church and we rather slavishly followed the Communion Service in the Book of Common Prayer. The vicar, who had come to dinner with us the night before, seemed ill at ease with the handful of elderly whites in his congregation and equally with the 50 or so blacks who were there. Our row of visitors sang lustily and, at times, it seemed as if only we were singing. I was asked after the service to bring 'my choir' again, as soon as possible. One minute before the service I was asked if I would preach the sermon. The vicar said that for the second time in his ministry he found himself with absolutely nothing to say. In the circumstances, and when I saw that he was speaking with the greatest seriousness, I agreed to do it.

I sat in my pew and listened to the two scripture lessons, framing my sermon as the words reached my ears. 'Arise and eat,' the Spirit of God said to Elijah and that was a good starting point. Eating is one of my favourite activities and the night before I'd had the most splendid meal with our farmer friends. 'And Elijah went in the strength of that meat 40 days and 40 nights,' said the scripture. And I still felt full from the previous night's repast so I could identify with the sated feelings that Elijah must have had. But then, of course, that allowed me to talk about the people in Malawi and Mozambique that I'd come to visit for Christian Aid who found it difficult to grow food and to eat. I could also appeal to my Zimbabwean audience's recent experience of drought and the difficulty of growing food at such times. I could underline my conviction that God wants us to enjoy the physical wellbeing that comes from eating well but, that beyond this, he shows himself to be the 'bread of life' which is so richly symbolised in our service of Holy Communion. My sermon lasted eight minutes and I sat down with, I'm bound to say, a feeling of some elation.

At two points only during the service did the liturgy move out of English and into the local Shona language. This was for the singing of the Sanctus and the Benedictus. We simply moved from one world into another. To hear Cranmer's florid prose in the high veldt of Africa is a curious experience. We did our best with it and, as I said, sang the hymns with great vigour. But there remained a certain degree of artificiality to the exercise for all that. The black people, I perceived, were barely participating in the liturgy at all. Then, when they opened their mouths to sing very softly the great canticles of the liturgy, we were lifted above the common level into the arena of heaven itself. There was rhythm, harmony and deep devotion, and a moment or two of mystical bliss. All that piety and experience of God had been locked up in these Shona people and was released momentarily in the singing of these two old hymns. The whole experience of going to church that morning was worth every minute for the sake of those divine Shona renderings of such ancient, revered words.

The other interesting experience of our stay here was a visit to the tobacco floors, where thousands and thousands of bales of tobacco are sold every day. Fortunes are made and it seems that the market for tobacco continues to be insatiable. The absence of smoking from restaurants and trains in Britain merely masks the fact that more and more tobacco is being consumed every year.

The climax of my stay here was the dinner party given by Richard and Elizabeth in my honour on the Monday evening. To it were invited Methodist leaders and other ecumenical figures from the churches in Zimbabwe. There were 17 of us and all the stops were pulled out to honour the visit of the President of the

British Methodist Conference. We had some marvellous conversation, with Crispin Mazobere regaling us with stories from Shona folklore, and Di and Mike Auret giving us some interesting insights into human rights in Zimbabwe during and after the war. It was marvellous to be able to see Paul and Joanne Kellner, both Colonels, who lead the Salvation Army in Zimbabwe. We worked together for a couple of very meaningful years in Haiti in the late 1970's. Richard brought out some of his best wines and the whole evening was a magnificent occasion. I don't think I'm likely to have another such dinner in my honour again.

Well, that's Zimbabwe. Now for the most intriguing part of my itinerary, Mozambique.

Dear Margaret

I arrived in Maputo from the luxurious life style of a British High Commissioner in Zimbabwe. What an enormous contrast I experienced! I've been staying in a guest house owned by the United Methodist Church. It's a homely but basic place. Whilst there I've been sharing a room with a string of Methodist pastors who've come in from remote parts of the country to do business in the capital city. They all had one thing in common: none of them spoke a word of English. There's something eerie about saying 'good night' and 'good morning' to people who can't communicate with you. My smile has been made to work overtime as I've tried to convey by the look on my face all those things that are quite beyond my barely existent Portuguese.

This has meant that I've had precious little privacy over these last few days. And if ever there were a place where I needed my own space then surely Mozambique is that place. It's a country in chaos. Two little incidents will best illustrate what I'm trying to say.

After about three days here we went the 300 miles or so towards the South African border, to a place called Masingir. That trip alone gave me an idea of the size of this country. It's just a piddling little run compared with some of the distances which can be travelled. We were meeting a community of people who've come back from years of exile in South Africa in order to re-commence their lives in their home country.

The group of people who came to meet us shambled forward and every one of them was stoned, as drunk as newts. They brew a beer from easily available leaves and every one – men, women and children – had taken far more than was good for them. And this was at 10.30 in the morning! But what else can you expect? Like the Eskimos in Canada, the Aborigines in Australia and the indigenous people of North America, their

25

whole culture has been destroyed and alcohol is the Great Escape. Their lands are unproductive, they've become dependent upon food aid for the whole of their time in South Africa, and now the bottom has been knocked out of their lives completely. Poor people! There's so much to do in this poor benighted land.

The second incident was just as heartrending. Travelling through the streets of Maputo, we came across what looked like the body of a teenage boy lying face down in the street. Not a single person was taking any interest in it. Cars were swerving to avoid it and life was going on as usual. Our journey took us about half an hour away into the outskirts of the city. We had an hour or so's business to transact at the local seminary. And then our return trip. I simply couldn't believe that the young man's body was still lying in the street. The only difference I could note was that somebody had put some tree branches in front of it so that cars could be warned and take the necessary avoiding action. Is life that cheap in Mozambique? It seems so.

I've eaten more chicken this week than I care to imagine. When we were out in the countryside for three consecutive days we had a run of six meals when chicken was served to us (including one breakfast). Everyone has killed the unfatted chicken for us visiting prodigals. I believe I've eaten half the chickens in Mozambique in the week I've spent here. It's a curious thing that they are often served with chips. In addition to that, I've drunk the most ghastly concoction which passes under the name of 'coffee' that could be dreamed of. The granulated coffee they serve here is liberally mixed with chicory. There's no milk in Mozambique (or at least none that I've been aware of) and this coffee is served with a generous injection of sweetened condensed milk. It's gruesome. But it's all there's been, so I've drunk it.

The great find for me has been the Wesleyan Methodist Church. Their Bishop, Bernardino Mandlate, studied for a short while at Wesley House in Cambridge so, naturally, I was taken with him from the outset. He is a young man with a very bright mind that bristles with ideas for his church. It appears he was ordained one day and made a Bishop the next. Some of the older lags call him (affectionately) 'the boy Bishop'. His church is very small and has tended to be inward looking; he wants to turn it out to face its community. He has plans for a playgroup, a primary school, the education of citizens in their civic and voting rights, agricultural and livestock projects, and an upgrading of the theological and spiritual formation of all his ministers. From the point of view of Methodism, Mozambique is a little bit of a backwater. But at such a crucial time in this country's life, I'm hoping that this Bishop gets the backing of as many people as possible. He's a star in the firmament as far as the future of this place is concerned. I so enjoyed baptising a dozen children and young people whilst in his church last Sunday. I also helped him to confirm a further dozen and, what's more, I preached. My sermon was translated into the local African language, Shangani. I always feel on these occasions that the translated version sounds infinitely more exciting than my original English. How I wish I could speak just one of these African languages. They sound fun!

I'm bound to say that I had greater fears here for my health than in any other place I'd visited. Facilities are rough, to say the least. But what is my discomfiture compared to the bombed-out, war-torn, down-at-heels life lived by these lovely people? They've really had such a battering for well over a generation. They deserve nothing but the very best.

Well, that's all for this time. Next stop the new South Africa.

Dear Margaret

The journey from Maputo to Johannesburg was like the one from Port au Prince to Miami, from a world of abject poverty and chaos to a world of affluence and structure. Startling, to say the least. The journey I've taken to come here took 40 minutes, the one from Haiti to the USA takes 90. That short span of time takes you from one order of being into another radically different.

After days of very basic living and the constant fear of a stomach problem it's been a great relief to find myself in a comfortable hotel room at the centre of Johannesburg. I've taken a long bath and actually unpacked my suitcase and taken longer over my lunch than I usually do.

I've attended a whole session of the South Africa Council of Churches and had good conversation with its General Secretary, Frank Chikane. He's been such a courageous church leader through the critical years from 1987 and has often been in great physical danger. I was not surprised to discover that he's submitted his resignation from his present position. He feels his work is done and that he must now be ready to move on to other things. The talk here is that he is about to be offered the Ambassador's job in Washington. He certainly deserves it.

I was particularly touched by Frank's presentation of a paper arguing a need for a Truth Commission which would allow the victims of apartheid to tell their stories of injustice and suffering over a long period of time. It would also offer an opportunity to the perpetrators of oppression to make a clean breast of it. All this story telling would be coupled with a general amnesty. The important thing is that this would offer a formal way to deal properly with the past and face the future in a more liberated way. The proposal was undergirded by astute theological reflection; I've always felt that the Church in South Africa has been so good at underpinning its stance on various political and social issues by a carefully spelled out biblical and theological justification.

This evening I went out to a Methodist School where the whole of the Johannesburg district (under the leadership of its Bishop, my friend Peter Storey) was meeting for a retreat. I had supper with them and then, abruptly, Peter Storey announced that I was to address the hundred or so ministers gathered at their evening meeting. 'Just tell them a few things that are on your heart,' he said. And so I did. I told them about the roots of my passion for social justice, the importance of Haiti in my life, the significance of my long years of training in higher education, and of my ministry in the City of London. I did it with a fair sprinkling of jokes and we laughed long and merrily.

It was a splendid evening and I was driven back to my hotel by Mvumi Dandala who is the Superintendent of the Johannesburg Central Mission. In the car he agonised with me whether he should allow his name to go forward as Frank Chikane's successor. Approaches have been made to him and he feels deeply ambivalent, not wanting to leave his job at the Mission. I told him that he shouldn't hesitate. He has all the gifts necessary and I do hope that he will throw his hat into the ring and, indeed, be offered the post. He'll grace the job and will offer real leadership to South Africa over the years ahead.

I remember that the last time I was here was with the British-South Africa Conference, an event organised by Bernard Crick. Then, with parliamentarians, trade unionists, industrialists, journalists and church leaders from both countries, we considered the new South Africa as it looked likely then to develop. We discussed a Bill of Rights and various other things. We travelled out, on that occasion, on 'Black Wednesday'. When we left England the pound was in free fall, and by the time we got to South Africa, Britain had withdrawn from the Exchange Rate Mechanism. The Members of Parliament with us were receiving yards of fax and wondering seriously whether they should return to England. I thought it was terribly funny.

In the event, they stayed and the Conference was a very moving occasion as we expressed from our various points of view our confidence and commitment to the new South Africa based on democracy and freedom for all its citizens. Huge problems remain. Today I've heard that even now, with parliamentary authority firmly in the grip of the Africa National Congress Party, the strong hand of the white community remains firmly in control of the bureaucracy. This was described as an 'ugly fact' and 'hidden apartheid' by some members of the SACC Executive. We'll have to see how things develop in these fields too.

Well, there we are. I've been 23 days away from home, flown in nine aeroplanes, and slept in 13 different beds. Now home for the new Connexional year. I've missed you and can't wait to be back.

Dear Margaret

I'm sitting in a tent, not something I'm accustomed to. It's one of a large number of strangely assorted articles housing a huge multitude of people. This curious agglomeration of dwellings, a kind of canvas shanty town, is where the thousands of visitors to Deene Park (near Corby in Northamptonshire) have settled so that they can fall out of their camp beds and into the myriad events which, together, form the Greenbelt Festival, a multi-coloured and magnificent extravaganza celebrating Christianity and the Arts.

All kinds of weird and wonderful things are happening here. Among the weekend's events are a Holy Ghost Train, 'Nirvana and Grunge'; iconoclastic challenges to comfortable Christianity by a radical 'biker-preacher' named John Smith; Wild Goose worship led by John Bell from Iona; a fashion show, music from the most mysteriously diverse array of pop music groups that you could ever wish to hear; and a Passion Play acted out under the stars.

This year's Greenbelt has been dominated in the media by the arrival of former page three girl Samantha Fox. In the past, she exposed her unclothed body to the gaze of tabloid readers, whereas now, having become a Christian, she wants people to know about her new convictions. Hence her visit to this late Summer Festival. She sang a song entitled 'Naughty girls need loving too', which caused all kinds of ironic comment in the press. It doesn't seem much different in my mind to Charles Wesley's 'Harlots and publicans and thieves, He spreads his arms to embrace you all.'

So what am I doing here with all these symbols of a culture into the waters of which I've scarcely even dipped the edge of a toe nail? I can only answer by saying that I've been invited to come. I've done a seminar to about 80 people on the latest situation in Haiti. Also, I've addressed a very large crowd in a marquee throbbing with music emanating from events on both sides of us. My subject has been 'Politics is too important to be left to politicians.' I've been able to put forward the argument that those Christians who abstain from the political process on the grounds that it dirties their hands and compromises their faith are simply being unfaithful to the earthed theology of the New Testament and to a God who chose to speak his most definitive word through the incarnation. I've wanted to argue with force that Christians should have an unblinkered view of the nature of politics and be prepared to enter the fray in an admittedly secular and pluralist society with people of goodwill who may (or may not) agree with the Christian point of view. A purist and idealised view of the conditions which must prevail before Christians enter the political fray is simply a formula for abstention. And Christians who abstain deserve the political leaders and the wicked world that others will give them.

I've thoroughly enjoyed this particular seminar. It generated lots of discussion. And then finally, with Nigel Forde (of Radio 4's 'Bookshelf programme'), and Adrian Plass, (who looks a little older than 13¾ now), Jeremy Vines (who's interviewed me several times on the subject of Haiti for the BBC), and two others, a writing dramatist and poet, I've been able to discuss my favourite books and do some literary criticism before a rather intellectual section of the Greenbelt audience.

And so, in the end, I've found Greenbelt to be a most invigorating and stimulating experience. If I'd never come, I'd have thought of it in a stereotypical way as the kind of occasion that old squares like me could never cope with. When I came last year I was all buttoned up. I wore a posh blazer, collar and tie, neatly pressed trousers, and carried a briefcase with my papers in. I was hugely overdressed! This year I wore my corduroy trousers and open neck shortsleeved shirt and fitted in with the scenery magnificently. And there are so many thirsting, questing, interesting young people eager to explore the sorts of issues that I'm interested in. Quite simply, it was fun!

That brings me back to this tent where I'm writing this letter. Mark Booth, my colleague who in this year of grace is the acting Superintendent of the Finchley and Hendon Circuit, is here on his annual pilgrimage with a small number of people from the Finchley Church. His tent nestles under an enormous flag post from which flies a red flag, a symbol of Mark's independence of mind and determination to be his own person. Whilst I'm writing these lines, he's busying himself barbecuing the chicken which will form the main element of the meal we're about to share. What fun! What a smashing day I've had! I hope they invite me back to Greenbelt next year.

7th September 1994

Dear Margaret

Last week I wrote from a tent at the Greenbelt Christian Arts
Festival. This week I'm writing from rather a posh room on the
campus of Loughborough University. I'm here to give what is
rather pompously called a Prestige Lecture at the Annual Festival
of the British Association for the Advancement of Science. The
Lecture is called 'Science and Religion'. It took place at
lunchtime today and, to my great relief, went far better than I'd
feared.

Just before it began, a member of our Golders Green
Church who comes to this event every year, sidled up to me with
a sheepish look on his face and said, 'So you've come into the
lion's den, then?' When I responded with a rather weak nodding
of the head, he continued, 'I'm sorry that I can't be with you, I've
decided to go to another lecture!' That was rather encouraging,
wasn't it? When I looked in the official programme later to see
what other lectures he might have gone to, there was only one,
and that was entitled 'Bubbles, Boomerangs and Beer'.

So I faced an audience of 150. Peter Briggs, the Executive
Secretary of the British Association, was my Chairperson and he
was so generous in his introductory remarks that it sounded as if
he was reading my obituary. But I wasn't yet dead and delivered
my piece with as much verve as I could muster.

I suggested that the old debate between science and
religion was now rather sterile. I pointed out that religion (in the
Christian sense) had had two thousand years to shape a perfect
world for people to live in and, obviously, had not yet delivered
the goods. I went on to suggest that science too, nearly four
hundred years into its reign of glory, had not yet fashioned a
perfect world. I suggested that both science and religion at their
worst are triumphalistic, arrogant, and far too self-confident. The
time has come for far greater humility on the part of both.

I suggested that attempts to harmonise science and religion, whilst worthy, often felt like special pleading. I wondered why we weren't ready to live with what a 17th century sage called 'reality in all its rich multiplicity', or what another called, 'divided and distinguished worlds'. Empirical 'truth' surely has its proper place in the way we see and evaluate the world around us. But so too, I argued, do the 'truths' of religious experience.

I went on to suggest that science and religion, in humbler mode, need to set their agendas according to the palpable needs of suffering humanity. Then in the name of ultimate Truth, by whatever name we call it, we might be able to hope that religion and science together would set themselves the task of solving the complex problems facing human beings around the world.

After the lecture there was some very animated discussion indeed and I went off to give an interview in the BBC Radio car which was parked on the campus.

For two consecutive weeks now I have been able to go and set up my stall in a veritable market-place of ideas. I've tried hard to present a Christian standpoint in a context where all kinds of ideas are being peddled. I find this both intimidating and invigorating at the same time. I'm convinced that a greater readiness to take our understandings of faith into the meeting places of life creates not only a context within which better apologetics will be done but also better evangelism.

The other most interesting thing to note was that quite a number of people came to speak to me who claimed to be Methodists and who simply wanted to thank me for coming into their world in the way I had. They felt affirmed by my visit. I had a similar response when I was after dinner speaker at a rugby club dinner a year or two ago. I was the last person to speak and, by the time I got on my feet, people were rather drunk and bread rolls were being thrown around by people who were bored with the speeches that had preceded mine. I had a whale of a time, was able to say a word about the Christian faith that means so much to me, and tell some of my funny stories (not a single dirty one) and poke gentle fun at the two millionaire sponsors of the rugby club who'd been sitting on my right and on my left. It was hilarious and much appreciated. When I'd finished, I found people claiming to be Methodists queueing up with their diaries to see whether I was available for Church Anniversaries and the like well into the remaining years of this millenium! I do feel it's important to get out where people are, both to proclaim the message and also to affirm people in their work and leisure.

Well, now it's back from Loughborough down the M1 and home again for the first of my District Visits. I feel that the Presidential Year now begins in earnest. See you soon.

Dear Tim

I came down to the Oval Cricket Ground today and was just a stone's throw from where you live. It seemed strange to think of you in Cornwall having a lovely (but rainy) holiday.

I was invited with some friends to see a day's cricket. But all I saw was a covered wicket and steadily falling rain throughout the day. But it wasn't as bad as it might have been because the person who invited us had a hospitality box. So we had rather a grand time looking over the interesting historical parts of the ground and having a splendid lunch.

I didn't know there was a 'long room' at the Oval just as there is at Lords. I saw pictures of the great Len Hutton who scored his 364 not out on this ground in 1938. There was also a superb portrait of Jack Hobbs who, to my mind, is the greatest cricketer of all time, combining grace and elegance with awesome power.

I had my photograph taken beside a marble bust of W G Grace. I couldn't look at his cold countenance without remembering dear old Mr Parsons, grandfather of my long-time friend Richard Rees. I remember Mr Parsons in the 1960's (he was then 90) telling me that when he was a boy he had bowled W G Grace out at the nets in Gloucester. The great doctor had given young Parsons sixpence for his pains and this became part of the old boy's rich store of anecdotes until his dying day. Finding myself in this nostalgic arena, I couldn't help myself thinking back to some of my own cricketing exploits. Will I ever forget captaining the Pegasus Cricket Club in Burry Port? Or gaining a hatful of wickets with my square-armed leg spin in the Wesley House match against Westminster College in Cambridge? The poor old United Reformed Church students, still rather cluttered with Calvinistic theology, felt protected by inevitable grace from my cunning wiles. But I knew better. I pitched the ball atrociously wide, aiming at the rough kicked up by bowlers at the other end and managed to turn the ball in a way that would have caused Shane Warne to purr with pleasure.

I also remember bowling two perfectly flighted off-breaks at John Woolf who'd opened the batting for the England Schoolboys. He played my two deliveries with the circumspection they deserved. Then, my third masterly delivery disguised a humming leg-break which explored the same arc as the two previous balls. John covered up in the same way as the ball pitched and turned away from him finding the edge of his bat and moving off into the grateful hands of my slip fielder. I bowled about a thousand rubbishy balls that day. They are all now in the dark box of my mind's forgetfulness. But I'm sure those three deliveries will be vividly remembered until I finally lie on my death bed. Poetry in motion, that's what they were.

William Wordsworth talked about 'emotions recollected in tranquillity'. Well, you're getting a real dose of that today. I still think that when I retire I shall spend my summers travelling the picturesque county cricket grounds of England with my comfortable patio chair and my appetising picnic lunch. The sound of leather on willow in grounds where poetry might be written will cheer my ageing soul in the days of my dotage.

I hope your Cornish holiday gives you the rest and refreshment you deserve. As you'll gather from this letter, there's no lack of either as far as I'm concerned.

Dearest Ruth

I'm writing to my 'political daughter' to tell you about a fascinating day that I've just had. I've spent it in Brighton, but not on a motorbike with mods and rockers or hell's angels, though that wouldn't be a bad description of some of the people I've met. In fact I've been at the Annual Conference of the Liberal Democratic Party.

I'm trying to visit all three party conferences so that I can say 'well done' to all those people who roll their sleeves up and get stuck into the business of politics. They get a lot of stick (sometimes, no doubt, they deserve it) but without them our whole society would be so much poorer. As I've started to go around the country, I've been meeting Methodists engaged in political life from grassroots level up to County Council level. There's an awful lot of them, and I'm delighted that our Church plays its part in making the wheels of our community life go round. So it was in the spirit of affirming all those who still see public service as an ideal worth working for that I went to Brighton yesterday.

It was a round of meetings and, at the end of the day, I don't think I could have said 'hello' to one more person. But it was worth it. I had a lovely chat with Alan Beith who is now the Lib. Dem. spokesman on Home Affairs and, of course, a staunch Methodist. I also met Charles Kennedy, who has just retired as the Party President, and Simon Hughes, one of their most radical MPs. I had a chat with Alex Carlyle who shares with me an interest in the plight of some people with personality disorders. And I met again Sir David Steel who invited me to make a contribution to a fringe meeting on the subject of Haiti in the light of the American invasion there.

18 SUN. 17 aft. Pentecost.

West Yorks. District

10.30 Gomersal - Circuit Cov.
Service

Eph 1: 16-23 "
John 1:1-18 "Thou O Xt art all in all"

3.00 Thackley - Young
Adults Group

6.00 St. Andrews Luke 10:25-37
" The Good Samaritan".

19 MON. O 9.00 am Margaret 10.18 Wakefield

10.00 Meeting with Mins, etc.
2.00 Heptonstall - Heritage
4.00 Todmorden Project

Train 6.28 - 8.58

20 TUES. Victoria Brighton
9.32 — 10.48
10.32 — 11.46

Lib Dems Conf Xn Forum AGM
Ralph Scott Address, Meeting

Brighton Victoria
4.50 — 5.43

Car Log or Weekly Cash Account.

St. Matthew.   WED.   **21**

9.30 Kalk

6.00 for Dinner FCFC Moderator +
6.30 leaders of member Churches
27 Tavistock Square

THURS. **22**
10.00 Xian Aid - Meeting with
new appointed Ass.
Directors
12.00
4.00 Xian Aid Exec

* Rail Strike *   FRI.   **23**
9.30 Kalk.

2.00 Driven to Nottingham
(Mark)
7.30 Beeston Ecumenical Group
NOTTINGHAM & DERBY DIST

r. 6.49: s. 6.55   SAT.   **24**

Eph. 2:11-22 / Mark 8:27-34.
2.30 East Midlands Ministry
Training Course - Notts Uni
Built to Last
7.30 Queen's Hall Derby -
District Celebration

MK 1: 14-20
Discipleship.

I spoke to the Christian Forum. I must say it was a bit of a rag bag of a meeting all preoccupied with constitutional niceties. By the time they were ready to allow me to speak there were only about 12½ minutes left. But, with one of my 'elastic speeches' I managed to squeeze everything in that I had intended to say. In particular, I encouraged young Christians who were prepared to get their sleeves rolled up in the world of political activity. I suggested that Christians mustn't take a purist view of politics and, on the grounds that it might sully them, withdraw from the fray. If Christians hold back from involvement in political and social affairs, then they certainly can't complain about the leadership that's offered by others. I explained that I understood political activity by Christians to be entirely consistent with belief in a God who loved the world (not the Church) so much that he gave his only begotten Son for its salvation.

One student was so enraptured by this message that she clung to me for the rest of the day and insisted on taking me on a personal guided tour of all the stalls that were exhibiting their wares under the roof of the Conference Chamber. So I met green Liberals, young Liberals, Welsh Liberals, electoral reform Liberals, and Uncle-Tom-Cobbley-and-all Liberals. It was great fun.

I sat in for two debates including one very rumbustious one that proposed the abolition of the Monarchy. Lots and lots of kids your age were there intending to give the leadership a hard ride. They had false noses and flags and generally sought to make themselves attractive to the television cameras who were expecting this to be a lively debate. My companion ensured that I sat right in the middle of this rebellious crowd. It was a very exciting place to be.

In the course of the day I met Bruce Kent, who's campaigned hard and long for the abolition of nuclear arms. Now he takes a wider brief and, I was intrigued by this, has founded a little organisation called GROT which means Get Rid of Them. The Them in this equation means the Tories! He's a firebrand!

There was one person I missed particularly at Brighton. That was Mark Bonham-Carter who died three or four weeks ago. I had met him at both meetings of the British-South Africa Conference, the first in Cambridge and the second in Durban and had established a very good relationship with him. He was the Lib. Dem. spokesman on Foreign Affairs and, of course, the grandson of Prime Minister Herbert Asquith. He was a very gracious man and ready to help me to understand some of the nuances of foreign affairs that I would never otherwise have grasped. I honour his memory.

I shall be in Blackpool in a fortnight at the Labour Party Conference. I'll write to you with full details of that after the event. I'm looking forward especially to sharing a fringe meeting with Tony Benn and Ann Clywd. I'm still trying to get to the Conservative Party Conference; it's proving to be more difficult than getting into a Wimbledon final. But we continue to try.

Take care and keep smiling, your daddy loves you.

29th September 1994

Dear Mum

I'm sitting writing this on a speeding express train that's getting me back to London from Cardiff. What's more, I'm sitting in the comfort and splendour of a first class seat. It's all been paid for by HTV (Harlech Television).

I went down earlier today because I've been recording an interview that will appear towards the end of October in a series called 'Face to Faith'. It's been such an intriguing day. I should say that the interviewer and producer had previously met me in London for a 'working lunch'. The meal was magnificent but I had scarcely any time or energy to appreciate it. They were conducting an in-depth interview whilst I ate and both of them had notebooks on their laps. So when I got to Cardiff today, they were ready for me.

The set was simple and clear of fussy detail. The only concession to any aesthetic consideration was an arrangement of dried flowers called Honesty. Perhaps that was meant to be a visual reminder of what they wanted above all to incorporate into their interview.

I'm still amazed that the interview proceeded without interruption for 25 minutes and 30 seconds exactly and I simply told the story of my life. I examined the factors that had shaped my earliest consciousness and most of the subsequent developments down to the present day. But also I identified those springs of spirituality that nourish my soul and the burning passion I feel in my gut for a just and fair world. Whilst I was delivering my soul, three cameras in the darkened part of the studio were zooming in and out and swishing round the floor as a continuity man in the gallery gave them instructions. So now I await the opportunity to see how this programme looks when it appears next month.

Other people appearing in the series will be Bishop Rowan Williams of Monmouth and Dr Mushaq Ally, the director of the Islamic Studies Department at Lampeter. I really enjoyed being back in the Principality again. My spirit always rises when I sit in a train that plummets into the depth of the Severn Tunnel or in a car that soars over the elegant lines of the Severn Bridge. 'Croeso i Cymru' it says ('Welcome to Wales') and I believe it.

Before coming home the producer, Emyr Daniel, took me to the little house where Ruth and her fellow students are spending this academic year. Emyr hails from Carmarthen and we had some marvellous conversation together. I didn't realise that he knew rugby player Caerwyn James personally. James was my boyhood hero. I was totally and utterly convinced that he deserved the Welsh outside half spot far more than his rival Cliff Morgan. But in those days when kicking to touch had so much more importance in the unreformed, prehensile days of rugby, James was doomed to be pushed aside. But his magic was patent and found its full expression in Barry John, his protégé, who regaled us all with his majestic rugby a generation later.

But I was distressed to hear how Caerwyn James had had to cope with his sexuality (he was known to be homosexual) through most of his adult life. It seems that his efforts to repress his sexual drives made him deeply unhappy and, when he died in his bath whilst spending a few days in Amsterdam in the early 1980's, the depth of his misery had reached its crushing and culminating point. So this lovely man, who brought such glory to the British Lions Rugby Team that toured New Zealand in 1971 and such poetry to a game where brute force always threatens to rule, carried his own inner tragic forces with him to the grave. How sad.

Well, I'm sorry to end on such a depressing note. I thought it was time I dropped you a little line. Ruth is in extraordinary good cheer and I'm so happy that she's chosen to study in my native heath. Lots of love.

5th October 1994

Dear Margaret

I am writing this from Blackpool. What a crazy cash-till kind of a place this is. It's absolutely crammed with people and they all seem to be going somewhere, though I couldn't begin to guess where. All the shops look like gaming machines, offering a bewildering combination of flashing lights, seducing visitors with pockets full of cash to come and spend their money on the trivia they offer.

The whole seafront is dominated by two enormous monuments. First, of course, is the Tower – one hundred years old this year and painted a garish gold to mark the anniversary. And the other is the new big dipper in the nearby amusement park. You have to be made with insides of steel even to look up at it. Quite what kind of a constitution you require to pay a large amount of money for the de-gutting experience of riding it I can only begin to imagine! Its main feature is that, after taking for ever to reach a mountainous height you then plunge at the speed of light (it would seem to me) on a vertiginous path that not only pitchforks you downwards but also turns you 90 degrees in the process. I can't think where people find their stomach linings and sang froid again after such an experience. Blackpool by the sea is, without doubt, a unique experience.

I'm here for the Labour Party Conference. Just an hour or two ago I spoke at a fringe meeting run by the Christian Socialist Movement. First to speak was Tony Benn. I first heard him speak in Cardiff over 30 years ago when he was Labour's bright young prospect. He's still extraordinary clear eyed (I speak of his physical rather than political sight) though he is now somewhat deaf. He spoke to me very knowingly about Methodism and its influence on 20th century politics.

When he rose to speak, he had his little tape recorder registering every word. Also open on the table in front of him was his mobile phone. It's quite extraordinary to think how he has used his tape recorder to capture his memories of all that was said in the closets of Cabinet as well as on the fringe of a Party Conference. He must feel that, when he opens his mouth to speak, what he says needs guarding and polishing for posterity. Certainly he was bright and bubbly in the talk he gave today. He talked about the practical importance of biblical pictures of peace and contrasted that with the mess religions have made of the quest for a peaceful society. 'Religion begins with a faith,' he said, 'but ends with a Byzantine bureaucracy.' And at another time he talked about 'the flames of faith' and how too many faiths had turned that flame into a readiness to burn others who either had different faith or none at all. But he was very generous in recognising the contribution of religion to the shaping of a civilised society. He even suggested, I don't think entirely flippantly, that someone with theological skills would be a very useful member of government in these days when religion is such an important component of so many of the world's problems.

Also speaking was David Clark, the Shadow Defence spokesman, and a member of CSM. He had the difficult task of speaking about peace and justifying expenditure on armaments. He made a reasonably good fist of it but in a not-very-memorable way.

I decided to answer the question of the day, 'Is God a peacemaker?' with a direct answer. I said, 'No, he isn't.' If he were, he'd have to explain upon what basis he chose to intervene to bring peace to some places whilst it was so manifestly absent in others. I suggested that there are many biblical images that show the kind of peace that is part of God's being and, indeed, God's will for the world. But we human beings are the peace-makers and we should spare no effort in working for peace. The essential step to take is the one that moves people from feelings of insecurity, which they defend by aggrandising or over-protecting themselves, to trust, where they see the other person, from any ethnic or cultural or national background, as someone to work with rather than to fight against. Christian teaching had a great deal to contribute in helping people move in this way from the mode of insecurity to that of trust.

Well, this is becoming quite an epistle. Its heavy seriousness contrasts with the glitter and the bright lights of the Blackpool I'm looking at through the window of the lovely room I've been given in the Church of the Sacred Heart. The Jesuits have always been so generous to me. It's lovely to be here and to be able to walk to the Conference and to the various meetings on the fringe. This comes with all my love.

My dearest Ruth

I'm writing this from home when I'd rather expected (or at least hoped) to be writing it from Bournemouth. I've been to the Liberal Democrat and Labour Party Conferences and have moved heaven and earth to try to attend the meeting taking place currently of the Conservative Party. But, alas, to no avail!

As you know, I felt that there was some point in rising above my partisan left-of-centre political position in order to say a word of encouragement to Methodists (and indeed Christians) involved in politics across the spectrum. I've only partly succeeded in that plan. But I'm bound to say, that, though my head had planned to visit all three, the Tory Party Conference would have taxed my diplomatic gifts to the utmost.

I've just sat watching the Home Secretary perform his annual ritual. Against a true blue background, he has mouthed his ritual dismissals of some of the weakest members of our society. He wants to punish people more severely, to crack down on crime, to control people's lives in a more strait-jacketed way. I must say there's something rather odd about this in my mind. It seems to run against Tory party philosophy. Isn't it they who believe that the market shall decide every argument? Don't they talk about getting government off people's backs? Aren't they concerned more than anyone else about the freedom of the individual? Don't they talk about choice all the time? Well then, why don't they let people do what they like? Why shouldn't criminals get away with it if they can? Why should government interfere with that interplay of supply and demand which should surely apply as much to the activities of criminals as anybody else? If the State chooses to interfere in that sector of our national economy and activity called 'crime' then why shouldn't the State interfere in other sectors of our national life? But there we are, the Conservatives don't really think in straight lines do they?

Enough of my ranting and raving. I'm very disappointed that some people have heard me speak against the Conservative Party and, therefore, felt that I shouldn't attend their Conference. They can't distinguish between my views on particular matters of policy and my readiness to accept the work of people of goodwill in whatever part of our political life they're to be found. Perhaps I'm expecting a degree of sophistication that is unreasonable. But it's still very sad.

On an entirely different note, let me say how much I'm looking forward to my two forthcoming visits to Wales. I've been working hard (with a friend) to translate a sermon into Welsh so that when I visit the Cymru District I can preach a whole sermon in the language of the land of my fathers. So how disappointed I was to discover that there will be sufficient English-speaking people present at the service in Llanfair Caereinion to make it inappropriate to preach entirely in the language of Dafydd ap Gwylim. Never mind, there'll be so much Welshness dripping out of my fingertips before long that I'll be inoculated against every kind of winter bacterium known to the wit of man.

This comes with all your daddy's love.

My dearest Ruth

It's been such an odd morning. I've sat in the room of the Secretary of Conference and chaired a meeting of about ten people. It was billed 'Meeting with the Archbishops'. And there, supported by various secretaries and officials, were the Right Reverend and definitely Right Honourable George Carey, Archbishop of Canterbury, and the equally Right Reverend and assuredly Right Honourable John Habgood, Archbishop of York.

It was my job to keep the agenda buoyant and to save it from being dragged into a bureaucratic consideration of the relationship between our Churches. I quite enjoyed the task! 'How could we introduce notions of generosity, imagination and vision into our ecumenical dialogue?' I asked. 'How do we keep faith with all the members of LEPs (Local Ecumenical Projects) who have struggled faithfully with ecumenism on the ground, sometimes for generations, and now are waiting for the sound of the trumpet and the clarion call from their denominational leaders?' We had a most interesting time.

It's still hard to believe that I'm keeping the company of such people as these Archbishops. It's three years now since I attended the enthronement of George Carey in Canterbury Cathedral. I shall not easily forget the pomp and the splendour of that occasion. And, more recently, I've shared the leadership of worship with the Archbishop in Westminster Abbey when he preached and I led some prayers in a service to give thanks for the life of Labour leader John Smith. As for John Habgood, he had just announced his impending retirement and speculation is rife about who will succeed him. I wouldn't mind the job myself!

This week I've received a letter from a fellow minister who announces his resignation from our ministry. Another has written to be reinstated after a few years outside the ministry. Yet another has written with news of a five year old child with severe learning difficulties and a personality disorder asking whether the needs of such a child can be given special consideration when a new appointment is found for him. And another comes from someone who's been writing to succeeding Presidents for a long time now with a local matter that he's become obsessed by. One letter thanks me for a sermon I preached at a Circuit Rally recently and another for the input I'd given to some theological students in Cambridge. One correspondent asks me to write a special word to Methodist Scouters and Guiders. Another wants me to take greetings to the Church in Burma where he served as a missionary for a number of years. I mention these because this is the real world I live in, a world shot through with the colours of pain and joy, delight and suffering. These days when I meet Bishops and Archbishops and the like, I pray that I may never forget the world of people's needs and worries, the street-level world of my everyday existence.

Your term is already half over. It seems an age since I last saw you. I began with two Archbishops, let me end with another two. On Saturday, when I visit the Cymru District I shall spend time with the Archbishop of Wales. And then next Tuesday, I'm to have dinner with the Greek Orthodox Archbishop of Thyateira and Great Britain, his Eminence Gregorios Theocharous. The strange thing is that the Greek Archbishop was a contemporary of mine in Wesley House, Cambridge. He spent a year with us when he was a mere Archimandrite. It'll be lovely seeing him again.

Your daddy loves you. God bless.

24th October 1994

Dear Kath

I'm in Wales again – land flowing with milk and honey. To be precise, I'm writing from Powys, one of the ancient kingdoms of Wales. The place abounds with unpronounceable names: such as Llanfyllin, Llanfair Caereinion, Llanfair ym Mochnant and (tongue-twistingly complete) Rhosllanerchrugog. If that string of place names doesn't make your mouth water then I don't know what would.

With Christine Walters and Margaret I've been visiting the Cymru District of the Methodist Church and some of our work done through the medium of the Welsh language. My old college pal Martin Evans-Jones is Chairman of the District and it was marvellous to stay for part of our time in Wales with him and his wife Gwen. We were able to enjoy some splendid hospitality and, because the pace of this visit was less intense than some of the others, we even had time to spend an evening playing Scrabble and an afternoon climbing a mountain.

Something very odd happened to me during this visit. As Martin drove us from Chester station towards his home in Rhuthun, my spirits lifted as we crossed the border and saw the great sign that said 'Croeso', 'Welcome to Wales'. And I was genuinely thrilled to be home. The old Welsh word 'hiraeth', an untranslatable word that conveys the deep yearning of a Welshman living in exile for the joy of returning home, had been gnawing at my inner being. So I was genuinely delighted to be back.

But as my time in Wales rolled on, I discovered other feelings too. I became aware that I'm nursing a deep resentment and anger which, to all intents and purposes, I have no problem with when I'm away from Wales. But when I get back it rises to the surface again. It's all rather odd. I tried to spell out in two meetings I spoke at what might be the cause of this anger. My mother's family came from the Rhondda Valley. My grandfather was a coalminer and he and my grandmother, whilst at school, were amongst a whole generation of Welsh people who were refused the right to speak their native language. The whole of the Rhondda Valley ceased to speak Welsh and became anglicised by dint of official, imposed policy.

When my grandparents moved west during the years of the great Depression, they did so as English-speaking Welsh people. And they settled in Welsh-speaking Carmarthenshire. That's where I grew up, a member of the great Anglo-Welsh society. I learned a little Welsh at school but never became confident in it. When I went to university in Cardiff the issue of the Welsh language was politicised by the founding of the Welsh Language Society. Then, people who'd been my friends at school wanted nothing further to do with me. I and people like me were considered second-class citizens. We didn't speak the language of the Bards and we were letting our culture down. So we were punished twice for the same thing. First we were robbed of our language by government policy, and then judged and found deficient by our fellow Welshmen who had escaped the implications of that policy.

No wonder my anger has never abated. It's certainly not helped by finding communities of Welsh speaking people who are so navel-gazing and self-indulgent about the way they consider Welsh culture that, purporting to be the guardians of their precious language and culture, they are actually building huge walls around it and are in the very process of administering a death-sentence to it.

I've been wrestling with all of this during my stay in Wales. Thank goodness Martin is a friend and that he and Gwen were more than ready to recognise my symptoms and help me deal with them. Isn't it a curious thing? In England, there's no one more ready than I to shout the odds and bring Wales to the attention of anyone who'll give me a hearing. Back in Wales, I get all twisted up about it. What a curious creature I am!

The issue of the language and culture apart, the autumn season in Wales showed a magnificent range of colours and they were seen at their best in the lovely sunlight we had on Sunday. When I'm back in London I'll remember Wales with unalloyed joy. Distance lends enchantment to any view, especially your native land.

Take care. See you soon.

23 SUN. 9 bef. Christmas.
One World Week begins.
Summer Time ends.

Ps. 27 : 1 - 8

Mt. 5 : 13 - 16

Mt. 13 : 31 - 35

Cymru Díst

10.00 Llanfyllin

Light / Salt / Leaven

Mk 9 : 2 - 29

1st and last
sections
bi-lingually

6.00 Llanfair Caereinion

The Mountain and the Valley

24 MON.

10.30 Bathafarn - meeting with
Mans etc,

Train -
Chester
2.39 — 5.39

25 TUES.

9.30 Kalk

12.00 Press Conf. - Anti-Slavery Int
Fr. Paraison

8.00 Dinner Arch. Gregorios

Thyateira House.

WED.   **26**

11·00 MCOD Central Committee
(margaret from work)
7·00 Wesleys Chapel - NCH Action
+ Reception   forch. Service)
                              Monks)

☾ 4.44 pm   THURS.   **27**

(with Stuart Owen)
6.00 Tea with Martyn + Lilly Allies
7·30 Caversham Height - One
                  world week

SOUTH WALES *and Jude.*   FRI.   **28**
DISTRICT   Padd   Cardiff
            9·00 ——— 11·00

12·00 District Women's Luncheon
5·30 Cardiff Meth Soc   Club
            Personal faith + Public life

r. 6.49: s. 4.40   SAT.   **29**

10·15 MHA - Penarth

2·30 Treforest - District Event
        Methodist Spirituality
      "Old Lamps for New"

1st November 1994

My darling Ruth

I'm writing to you in the hope that these few moments spent in your company will calm me down a little. I've just had a parking ticket and I'm pretty fed-up about it!

You know that I'm going to Burma (I should be accurate and call it Myanmar) in a couple of weeks' time. This information is public knowledge, it appears boldly on the green prayer cards that have been distributed across the length and breadth of the country. That means that every single person in Britain who has ever been to Burma (that's how it seems) wants me to convey greetings or even take little presents with me for friends they once knew there. I think that's absolutely charming. But there's one snag. I don't remember when I was last so busy. So when someone asks me to take some money to help a clinic in Burma I have to find time to go to the bank to turn a few English pounds into American dollars. And that's the kind of operation I'm finding it extraordinarily difficult to find time for.

This year, your poor old mother has had to mow the lawn right into November. She comes home from work and gets straight out on to the grass. Or else, as the days have grown too short to allow that, she has had to use her precious weekends to do it. And now, even worse, the leaves are falling off the trees and need raking and sweeping and being disposed of. So poor old mum is somehow having to find the energy for that. When I come home from a long weekend away and find three days correspondence waiting for me and a whole fistful of other contacts demanding my attention, there simply isn't any time for the ordinary common-or-garden tasks that represent my contribution to the smooth running of this household.

My hair has grown so long (at least at the back) that I think I must be starting to look like one of those rare breeds of sheep that you see on posters in the Lake District or North Wales.

58

There hasn't even been a little corner in my diary where the barber could have got his shears out and put me in the position where, like a sheep before his shearer, I 'opened not my mouth'.

Mum's been screaming for her house keeping money and I haven't had time to organise it. My bank statement arrived and, for the first time in yonks, I haven't brought my accounts up to date. And now this parking ticket. In order to make this transaction in the time I have available between now and my departure to Myanmar, instead of going to the bank on foot as is my wont, I decided to go by car. I left the car where I shouldn't have done and I've paid the price. As well as the bank's commission for turning pounds into dollars I've had to add £30 of my own, which makes a total tariff of something like 33%. I wanted to scream when I saw that plastic bag containing the traffic warden's little message for me.

On a happier note, I did actually keep a whole evening free for your mother's 50th birthday. The evening was squeezed between my visit to the Convocation of the Diaconal Order in Swanwick and the Lay Workers' Conference in High Leigh. But it was great for the two of us to spend a whole evening together. We went out to the lovely fish restaurant in Mill Hill and had griddled halibut with fresh vegetables, washed down with a bottle of Muscadet (*sur lie,* of course).

I don't know how many people have told me that mum looks just the same age now as she did years and years ago. But the fact is that she has now joined me on the other side of the half century threshold. Between us we total 102 years! Thus we take one step at a time towards our eternal destiny. Hasn't it been a year of great events? The Presidency of Conference, 25 years of marriage, and now your mum's 50th birthday. And yet we're still alive to see each other's face and to rejoice for as long as the day *is* the day.

This comes with all my love. I miss you terribly. .

11th November 1994

My darling daughter

You'll never guess where I've been this morning. I've been to number 10 Downing Street, but not to meet your friend the Prime Minister! I've been to what's called the Crown Appointments Office to meet a senior civil servant whose job it is to appoint Bishops and Archbishops and all the company of heaven. In fact, the present holder of this office is named John Holroyd who's a former pupil of Kingswood School (your own Alma Mater). He met me and the Secretary of Conference and was genuinely anxious to explore our minds about possible contenders to succeed the Archbishop of York. He actually wanted us to 'talk-up' candidates we would feel comfortable with and to give a thumbs down to those who definitely registered number eight on the episcopal Richter Scale. We were most anxious, naturally, that an appointment should be made which would, as far as possible, combine the intellectual skills of Dr John Habgood with his commitment to ecumenical relations.

It's a funny old thing being in a lovely office in Downing Street as a Methodist minister helping to choose someone who will be a pillar of the establishment! It's even more ironic that the Crown Appointments' Officer should be himself a Methodist although now layered over with an Anglican veneer.

As I left the office to go down the stairs I bumped into a huge gang of press people waiting for the arrival of President De Klerk of South Africa. I was told that a cleaner had left earlier this morning with a Harrods' plastic shopping bag. Just at the moment the owners of Harrods are of course implicated in allegations about certain Government ministers selling their services for money. So any overt connection between Downing Street and Harrods is viewed with great suspicion, or even seen as evidence of connections between the Al Fayed brothers and the Government that could turn into a juicy tabloid story.

Whilst on the subject of ex-Kingswood pupils, I should just tell you of someone I met 48 hours ago. Not in Downing Street this time, but in Brussels. I was over there with the Moderator of the United Reformed Church to visit key people who function within the Byzantine workings of the European Union. We met a number of members of the European Parliament and also people in planning and policy units of various kinds.

One of the most interesting meetings we had was with Sir Leon Brittan's 'Chef de Cabinet', the man who co-ordinates the seven-person advisory unit that works with their European Commissioner to achieve his policy objectives. In this case, the person was Mr Colin Budd. Before we'd begun to talk about Europe and policy and the like, he declared quite openly that he was a Methodist, the son of a Supernumerary minister, and also a former pupil of Kingswood School.

Just at the moment there's some excitement in Brussels at the fact that Neil Kinnock is due to arrive to take up his position as European Commissioner with responsibility for transport. It's thought that he's going to become one of the most powerful Commissioners because of his links with the German Democratic Socialist President of the Parliament (to say nothing of the fact that Glenys, his wife, is a member of that parliament), and also with Pauline Green who heads the Socialist group in Parliament.

It appears that the Parliament is destined to become increasingly important in the working of Europe and that Neil Kinnock may find himself on a rising tide. Apparently he and Sir Leon Brittan, between whom you'd have thought there was precious little in common, get on like a house on fire. Neil gave a little speech at a dinner a week or so ago where he announced that the only two things that Sir Leon and he had in common were a British passport and a love of opera! Then he went on to endorse in glowing terms the work of Brittan and gave a fulsome promise that he would support his fellow British Commissioner with some real commitment.

Colin Budd was very forthright about some aspects of European Union life. He described one of the Commissioners (who's given those of us working in non-Governmental organisations a great deal of concern for some time) as 'not far from certifiably nuts'. Nor did he know whether the Commissioner's successor, would do any better. Colin Budd was very clear that the European Union was achieving the two objectives that had originally been set in the dim and distant day of the Treaty of Rome, namely peace in Europe and the promotion of prosperity. Now, in his opinion, the agenda must move forward to consider economic union, defence and political union.

Most people working for Britain in Brussels are fed-up with the Tory administration that completely undersells the vision of Europe and undermines the work of people like Sir Leon Brittan and Bruce Milan, our Commissioners there. Colin Budd's also pretty fed up that regulations about straight bananas and the sale of aspirin and the quality of mincemeat should be taken by the tabloid press (at the populist end) and leading members of the CBI (at a loftier level) as being the defining experience of European togetherness. He was also very forthcoming about the way the tabloid press in Britain love to vilify Jacques Delors, the President of the Commission. Who can ever forget the editor of the 'Sun's' headline 'Up yours, Delors' from two or three years ago? In Brussels, however, again to quote Mr Budd, 'Mr Delors walks on water.' His thinking is precise, challenging and pregnant with possibilities for a new climate for European peoples to live in.

Well, I hadn't intended to go into all that. I merely wanted to show you how, like the Holy Spirit, ex-pupils of Kingswood School go where they will and turn up in all kinds of odd corners from the sprouting Brussels bureaucracy to the inner sanctums of Downing Street.

This comes with all my love as always.

18th November 1994

My darling Ruth

Two great events within four days of each other and I simply have to write to tell you all about them. First of all, the solemn and imposing commemoration of all our war dead at the Cenotaph on Remembrance Sunday. It was simply awe-inspiring to be present at such an occasion. The protocol and the sense of ceremony were impeccable. The Queen and her family arrived on the little chalked marks showing where they were to stand in the middle of Whitehall just five seconds before Big Ben struck eleven. The massed bands were there, playing haunting and emotive music. Your mum was in a crowd of other distinguished ladies on a balcony in the Foreign Office behind us. I stood with other religious leaders immediately underneath her. On my right was my old pal John Newton (we were both wearing our London PhD convocation gowns) and on my left the Chief Rabbi, Jonathan Sachs. It was deeply moving, in the simplest of simple rituals, to bring to mind all those countless people who had died in the various wars of this century. May we never trivialise the country for which they made the ultimate sacrifice.

Then, on Wednesday, and this was only made possible by the cancellation of my trip to Burma, I attended a reception given by the Speaker of the House of Commons to mark the State Opening of Parliament. In the most magnificent set of rooms looking out over the River Thames a goodly and motley crowd of politicians, worthies and the *hoi polloi* like me met for an hour just after the Queen had left the Palace of Westminster to go to her other (Buckingham) Palace.

Out of these two great events I have culled some memories that I shall long treasure. In the Foreign Office on Sunday, for example, I met that old bruiser, Ian Paisley. He beamed at me when I was introduced as the President of the Methodist Conference and assured me that he read the 'Methodist Recorder' without fail every Thursday. He even said that he

63

looked at my column (notice he *read* the 'Methodist Recorder' and *looked at* my column!). It was quite clear to me from the way he addressed me that his conversation with me was perfunctory. I know he has little time for us deviant Methodists.

But what was interesting was the chat I had with Jim Molyneaux four days later in the Speaker's House. This leader of the Unionist Party told me (without my asking) that he'd searched out a corner of the Reception that was as far distant as possible from his old protagonist, Ian Paisley, who was lurking somewhere else at that moment. 'All Paisley ever does,' said Molyneaux, 'is declare himself to be against every proposal that's made. That's the course of action that taxes his tiny brain the least. When I think of all those hours through the night that I and others have laboured over the Northern Ireland Peace Agreement and the endless negotiations about the ceasefire and the eventual participation of the IRA in talks, it makes my blood boil when I hear Paisley just open his mouth and dismiss everything that's proposed. But his days are definitely numbered,' he continued. 'About a third of his support is from out-and-out fundamentalists, another third from young people who see him as their champion in some blinkered kind of way, and a further third who waver between those two positions. When he had the audacity to call me Judas Iscariot because I had aligned myself with the peace process, he definitely alienated numbers of his fundamentalist supporters. And his heavy-handed opposition to the peace process in general runs the danger of losing his more progressive and youthful support. And he knows that. But he doesn't know what to do about it. We may be near to the end of Paisley's role in modern Irish history.'

I found this all terribly interesting. Jim Molyneaux also told me that when a television company had come to do a profile of him, a journalist asked him how he felt to hear Ian Paisley compare him to Neville Chamberlain (the great appeaser). 'I tried to look crestfallen,' said Molyneaux. 'I told the journalist that, when you've been compared to a follower of our Lord one week, it was hard to be compared to a mere former Prime Minister the next.'

At the Foreign Office, I also met Michael Howard, the Home Secretary. You know that he and I were at school together. But that didn't prepare me for his assault. 'Leslie,' he declared with some animation, 'how lovely to see you. When you're on the radio I listen avidly to your every word. I don't agree with a quarter of what you say but I never miss a word.' I replied that I followed his progress just as closely as he obviously did mine. And I added, 'I don't agree with much of what you propose either.' He laughed and insisted that his wife meet me and was delighted himself to meet mum.

With Rabbi Jonathan Sachs I discussed the way religious leaders can together identify an agenda that helps the nation to consider moral questions and ethical issues. I admire him enormously for the contribution he's made in this regard. He seems to have sprung out from being a Jewish leader to becoming a national leader in his own right. It was clear to me from the way the Prime Minister spoke to him, addressing him frequently by his first name, that John Major thinks so too. When the Prime Minister winked at me and said that he'd been asked by the Chef de Protocol to go and head a queue to lead people to their appointed places, he couldn't have been surprised when I retorted that I'd follow him on this occasion but that he mustn't take that to mean that I'd go wherever he led. He chuckled.

After the Cenotaph ceremony I had the chance to talk to David Hope, the Bishop of London. I had read that he was 'kicking the diocese around a bit' in order to get its affairs straight. I wanted to know just how radical he intended to be. He means to abolish the Area Synods which currently meet under the Chairmanship of each of his Suffragan Bishops. And also, for the moment, he has no intention of pressing for a replacement for the recently deceased Bishop of Kensington. He wants the Diocesan Synod to relate as closely and intimately as possible with parishes or 'clusters of parishes'. He's challenging all budget lines and is really determined to lick London into shape. I really do wish him well.

Last week Brian Beck and I were in consultation with the Crown Appointments Office on the question of a successor to Dr John Habgood as Archbishop of York. In my mind, I was very clear that David Hope is a clear and logical successor. But it may count against him that he's only just been in the capital city long enough to begin the kicking around exercise. It may be considered necessary to leave him there for a while longer.

I spoke at both my great occasions with a number of High Commissioners. Dr Francis Ngoni, from Zimbabwe, is of course a member of our Golders Green Church. The Sierra Leonean High Commissioner was recently at a memorial service where I preached for Bankole Timothy. The Kenyan, Botswanan, Ghanaian and Tongan High Commissioners all had animated conversation with me because various members of their staff are also members of the Church. Indeed, some of these heads of mission have themselves attended from time to time. It's a great privilege to feel that I can have this degree of contact with the world at large through the membership of our Church.

John Redwood, Minister of State for Wales, introduced himself to me. When he heard who I was he at once volunteered the information that he is an old boy of Kent College, Canterbury, a Methodist School as he proudly declared. I found it quite difficult talking with Mr Redwood because, of course, he has openly boasted that he's never so much as spent a single night in Wales! When I visited there two or three weeks ago, people in the Principality, not just the nationalists either, declared themselves really fed up with a Government that makes such insensitive appointments. So, when we'd talked for a couple of minutes about Kent College, I suggested to Mr Redwood that I could put him in touch with someone who'd teach him a little Welsh. He looked very shy at the suggestion and, conveniently, saw someone out of the corner of his eye to whom he addressed himself forthwith.

I could go on talking about the little chats I had with a number of other people. The newly appointed Lord Mayor of London, the Lord Lieutenant of Sussex, Betty Boothroyd's next door neighbour, Secretary of State for Defence, Malcolm Rifkind, Canon Michael Mayne of Westminster Abbey (Chaplain to the House of Commons), and that old Methodist bruiser, Sir Rhodes Boyson. They were all fun. As too was Sir Isaac Sternberg who is the President of the International Council for Christians and Jews and who has done fantastic things to enhance relations between our two religions. I fully expect to be in touch with him again and, no doubt, I tell you all about that some other time.

Well, as you stick your nose down into your books and write your endless essays about the European Union and French culture, I hope you don't mind me going on a bit about these recent privileges that have fallen my way. I now see what holding this particular office can do to create opportunities for dialogue with those who hold power in the affairs of the nation and make decisions that shape people's horizons. And I've enjoyed every single minute of it.

This comes with hugs and kisses from your silly old daddy.

23rd November 1994

My dearest Ruth

Last week I felt impelled to write to you about how I fared with the *glitterati* and the *literati* who gathered in the state rooms of the Speaker's House in the Palace of Westminster. This week I'm writing from the spare bedroom of the Methodist manse in Golders Green; I'm on altogether firmer ground. I've been enjoying a time of pure bliss, ten whole days firmly rooted at home, brought about because (for some reason or other) the Myanmar Government considers me *persona non grata*.

Blaise Pascal (17th century French philosopher, scientist and theologian) is one of my great thinkers of all time. I hope your French studies are not so focused on the business and commercial use of the language that you don't have time to meet those who've forged it and explored its possibilities to the uttermost. From time to time, Pascal used to go to the Palace of Versailles to attend one or another of the great banquets or receptions or balls that took place there. King Louis XIV was known as 'The Sun King' and his state occasions were renowned for their splendour. Hundreds of candles lit up the state reception rooms and their light was reflected from the scores of huge mirrors that hung from the walls. Those who attended these functions, men and women alike, dressed up to the eyes in their livery and lace, the one out to impress and upstage the other. The French verb that perfectly describes it is *se pavaner* (to strut like a peacock); or else the phrase coined by André Gide, *endimanché jusqu'aux yeux* (Sundayed up to the eyes). It was all very grand. But it was also all very hollow.

Blaise Pascal used to imagine what all these important people looked like when the ball was over and they got to their bedrooms tired out. He pictured them carrying their candle to their chamber, putting it on a little table while they undressed in readiness for bed. Off came the frilly outfits, thrown over the back of a chair or else dumped in a heap on the floor. How daft they all must look in their underwear! How daft we all look in our underwear. Then these grand people, the great and the good, puffed out the candle and collapsed into their beds.

Now there was no one to impress with fine language and witty discourse. Now there was only darkness and solitude. How, wondered Pascal, did these people who thrived on strutting cope with being alone? Did they face the inner voice that came from deep inside them with as much confidence as they showed in their brilliant public conversation? For Pascal, the really important thing for any human being is to know that peace with oneself that is God's gift. All the social gifts in the world cannot mask inner emptiness forever.

Well now, all that arose from the fact that I've been home for this unexpected length of time. After all the fuss and the splendid occasions I've been enjoying so breathlessly over the last few months, it's been good to have some time with myself again. It's been so satisfying to be still for a while and to rediscover myself embraced by the sense of God's presence. Next week, of course, it'll be all go again.

I'm sure you don't mind your daft old daddy rambling on like this. Keep smiling. God bless.

My dearest Margaret

I am writing this from a hotel room (that's exactly what it is) on the campus of Warwick University. Last night I gave a lecture that is sponsored by the Universities of Coventry and Warwick, together with Coventry Cathedral. I spoke about 'Haiti fifty days after President Aristide's return'. There was a good number who listened avidly, and afterwards there were refreshments and finally a grand dinner for fourteen of us before the evening drew to its close.

The most searing memory of yesterday, however, was nothing to do with the lecture but more to do with my journey to Coventry. I left home at 7.45am with my usual two Presidential suitcases. They were a little heavier than usual because I was carrying more books than normal due to the demands of this particular weekend. I shut the front door behind me and walked the length of our street. You'll know the feelings I had as I saw four buses cross the end of the road roaring off towards the tube station.

I shuddered, knowing that inevitably meant a longer wait than I needed. When a bus eventually came, I was one among a couple of dozen to get on. It was already full and my suitcases got in everybody's way. We were standing like packed cattle on the downstairs deck and, at every stop before the station, passengers had to clamber over my suitcases. Many a suppressed imprecation was muttered at my expense and I was not a popular man. When I arrived at the tube station, I was aware that I was in danger of being late. There was an enormous queue at the ticket counter. I didn't have the right money for the machine and I had no alternative, therefore, but to stand in line.

When I eventually got to the platform, you'll have guessed it by now, a train was pulling out! It seemed an age before the next one came but, when it did, it was full on arrival and we were multitudinous on the platform. Once more my suitcases became veritable stones of stumbling for the serried ranks of harassed commuters. I managed to survive their barely suppressed contempt to Euston but now there were only five minutes before the Coventry train was due to leave. It's almost impossible to hurry up escalators with two suitcases at rush hour. I did my best and was quite breathless on arrival in the main station concourse. My train was going from platform 6 and, with one minute to go, I jumped aboard gratefully.

Now I've got to think of the last part of my journey home. I'm due to arrive back in Euston at 11.05pm on Monday. I honestly don't think I can cope with the thought of going down to the Underground and then waiting at midnight for a connecting bus in Golders Green. I think that just writing this letter to you has persuaded me that I shall be bold and charge the Connexion the price of a taxi home.

Keep smiling. See you Monday.

SUN. *3 bef. Christmas. 2 in Advent.*
4 *Bible Sunday.*

Manchester & Stockport District

Eph 2:11-22
10.30 Flixton - 100th Anni.
Mk 12:28-34 Building on Foundations

3.00 Timperley - Christians & Politics

Is 55:6-11
Luke 4:14-21
6.30 Timperley -
The Survival of Hope

MON.
5
10.30 Central Hall - meeting minis, etc
Train 12.30 MHA - Bowdon
Picc Euston 3.30 Manch Housing Ass Offices.
23 05 4.00 NW Fed - Training for Ministry
20.00 6.00 Hartley Vic. Students.

TUES.
6
11 am Keith.

3.00 Debbie Holmes - Shelter
5.00 - 6.00 Launch of 'Por la Vida'
[COLOMBIA]   House of Commons

Car Log or Weekly Cash Account.

WED   **7**

10.30
    Xian Aid Exec
12.00
2.00 First Meeting of New
                    Board

THURS.   **8**

12.30 Fiona & David Bidnell

☽ 9.06 pm   FRI.   **9**

9.30 Kalk.

NEWCASTLE ON TYNE DISTRICT
Kings Cross 15.00 — Newcastle 17.40
10.00 MHA Jesmond 55: s. 3.52   SAT.   **10**
11.30 " Cramlington

2.30 Benton - Christian Faith in
            the Modern World
7.00 Brunswick — The Servant King

My dearest Ruth

Last night I gathered with a hundred and fifty Friends of Wesley's Chapel in the Throne Room at Westminster Cathedral. This extraordinary year has taken me into so many interesting places where I wouldn't normally expect to see the colour of the carpet or the wallpaper! But this splendid room matched them all. Cardinal Basil Hume and Lord Wetherill (ex-Speaker of the House of Commons) were at the door to welcome guests to the Reception. There were food and drinks and a nice time for people to meet and mingle. I just wondered what dear old John Wesley would have thought of all this splendour. Dr Samuel Johnson thought that Wesley was a lovely man but regretted deeply that he never sat still long enough to engage in what, for Johnson, was the greatest social gift of them all – good conversation. I imagine that last night he'd have come and smiled a rather forced smile before taking his leave in order to write another page of his journal.

At the conclusion of the Reception there were some brief formalities. I was called upon to lead the final prayers and felt (the incurable urge of the Welsh) that I ought to say a few words. I indicated that whilst I was the present occupant of John Wesley's chair, I didn't think that that piece of furniture (a figment of the Methodist collective imagination) would bear any resemblance to the splendid golden, carved and scarlet-upholstered throne which dominated the room where we were gathered. Of course, I had to sit on it. That's what thrones are for. Several photographs were taken of the President pretending to be a king! It's interesting that the Cardinal told me he'd never himself sat on it, that it spoke the language of another age and of modes of Church governance that now, thankfully, were well done with.

I was able to point to the picture of Cardinal Manning which hung large on one of the walls of this splendid room.

Manning, together with General Booth of the Salvation Army and Hugh Price Hughes (the founder of the West London Mission), worked together at the end of the 19th century on the issue of Temperance. They also combined well together to help mediate in the 1889 dockers' strike. It was nice to be able to make some Methodist/Catholic tie-ups in that way.

When the time came to leave last night's Reception, I felt I could understand just how Cinderella might have felt after going to the Ball. It was all a little larger-than-life and brighter-than-fairyland. I wouldn't have been at all surprised if a pumpkin pulled by mice had been waiting for me at the door. What an evening! What lovely fellowship now exists between our Churches.

17th December 1994

My dearest Ruth

Last time I wrote I was full of a recent visit to the Throne Room at Westminster Cathedral. This time it's the House of Lords. Is there no end to this Presidential gallivanting? The answer of course is, yes, in six months' time.

Last night was somewhat different. It was more personal. Lord and Lady Murray (Lionel and Heather to you) invited mum and me to dinner in the House of Lords and it was a lovely, intimate occasion. The dinner itself was good and the ambience was, of course, spectacular. Lionel continues to work hard on labour and social issues for NCH Action for Children, and is increasingly involved in campaigning for improved access to public places for people with disabilities. He has so much to offer and, where people like him are concerned, I quite see the point of a second Chamber that draws on such people's expertise.

Interestingly, there had been a debate earlier that day on the British Government's relationship with Myanmar (Burma). Lionel rose to put a question to the Minister for Overseas Aid, Baroness Chalker, asking whether she could use her good offices to discover why the President of the Methodist Conference (me!) had not been granted a visa to visit there recently. The Minister promised to investigate.

Whilst climbing the stairs to get to the dining room I bumped into Lord Mancroft with whom I work as a fellow trustee of the Addiction Recovery Foundation. It was lovely to see him and, especially, to urge him to do all he could to help the case of Adrian Garfoot, a medical practitioner in the East End of London who's been prescribing drugs to hard-core addicts as part of a very carefully thought-through programme for dealing with their problems.

Current medical wisdom suggests that such people should be given Methodone as a substitute for their drugs and that this should be reduced drastically within a very short period of time. Adrian Garfoot's contention is that this simply leads them back into the world of drugs and into criminality in order to secure a supply of the substances they require. He's got into trouble with the medical authorities and a tribunal is looking at his case. Their judgement will set precedents and, consequently, many people are awaiting the outcome with more than the usual interest. Benjamin Mancroft, a Tory hereditary peer, is himself a specialist in the area of drug dependency, having been addicted to heroin himself once-upon-a-time. He now contributes powerfully to debates in Parliament on this subject and is well-placed to influence people whose opinions might be important in a case like this. So we talked about that and he promised me that he was deeply involved and wanting the same result as I did.

Later on, I met Denis Howell, who in Harold Wilson's government, had been Minister of Sport and, wait for it, Minister of Weather. I remember how he was appointed when we were in the middle of a long drought. When the rains fell he was widely applauded as if he'd personally had something to do with it! He told me that during his tenure of that particular office there had been blizzards, floods and even an earthquake. He'd retired as the undisputed master of British weather. On one occasion, he told me, he'd been at the Cheltenham races with the Queen Mother. It had poured all morning and the Queen Mother had asked him to accompany her to inspect the horses before the two o'clock race in the afternoon. She told him that, as the responsible person, she expected him to arrange for the rain to stop falling before the race began. And, in fact, as soon as he and the Queen Mum put their feet upon the turf, the rain stopped abruptly. Her Majesty was distinctly more than amused. She urged the Minister to come the following day when the Cheltenham Gold Cup was to be run. He said he couldn't because there were questions to answer in the House. Imagine everybody's surprise, when, on the day of the great race, Cheltenham found itself under six inches of snow and the race had to be called off. The Queen Mother rang Denis Howell to tell him that all this had happened only because he had not been there himself.

I also met Lord (Geoffrey) Howe. It was Geoffrey Howe who'd served for a long time as Margaret Thatcher's deputy, and who finally made the devastating speech which brought about her downfall. He's a fellow Welshman, although you'd never tell that by listening to him. And, of course, it was he of whose assaults across the floor of the House of Commons Denis Healey had said that it was the equivalent of being 'savaged by a dead sheep'. I found him much more animated than that. When he heard I was from Llanelli he put on his loudest Port Talbot accent and we had a lovely moment or two together.

He told me how, when he was Foreign Secretary, he paid the first visit to Czechoslovakia in the days following the fall of the Berlin Wall. The Prime Minister of that country took Howe and his party out for dinner to a Bohemian restaurant where they had a wonderful evening. A gypsy violinist, who Geoffrey Howe thought looked uncannily like Nigel Lawson, played haunting and sentimental mid-European tunes all evening. When the meal was over the Czechoslovakian Prime Minister got up and danced and sang, and then invited the British Foreign Secretary to contribute in like manner. Geoffrey Howe was not caught napping. He'd brought with him copies of the words of Cwm Rhondda, 'Guide me, O thou great Jehovah', and got the whole party, British and Czechoslovakian, to sing this great valley tune in four-part harmony. 'Oh, we had a lovely time, boyo,' he said to me as we parted.

So you see we've had another smashing evening. I could get quite addicted to this Presidential style. Soon you'll be home for Christmas and you'll start puncturing my great big euphoria with your shafts of realism. I need you. Come home soon. Your daddy loves you.

Dear Jon

I'm just back from the 'Start the Week' studio and want to tell you at once how it all went. I approached this hour long radio programme with some trepidation. The invitation came because I'd given the Prestige Lecture at the Summer Festival of the British Association for the Advancement of Science on the subject of 'Science and Religion'. I avoided the normal approach to that subject and argued instead that since neither Religion nor Science seemed to be coming up with the goods, that is they had not yet delivered anything vaguely approaching a decent world for people to live in, it was time they got off their high-horses and took a look at the facts. They needed to be less triumphalist, less smug, less interested in scoring debating points off each other. Instead they needed to learn to listen to the deep yearnings of ordinary human beings who long for a world fit for them and their children to live in. This humility would make them allies rather than competitors, respecters of each other's integrity rather than denigrators one of the other, and at the service of humanity.

Well, that's what I tried to say last September and I gave a quick interview for Radio 5 Live who had a studio at the Festival. Someone in 'Start the Week' heard my lecture and wanted me to come on the programme. However, because the Presidential diary is cast in concrete, every single Monday since then I have been at some distant part of the compass. Consequently, it was only in the very last programme before Christmas that I was free to go on at all. I'm still astonished that they kept the spot open for me that long. But they did, and I've just done the job. I was terrified lest the subject might have gone cold and I would have little to say. But I needn't have worried.

Also on the programme was Susan Greenfield, who's Professor of Neuroscience at Oxford and who is giving this year's lectures for children at the Royal Institution. That's quite a feather in her cap and she is a magnificently lucid person. In addition, Bratibha Parmar, a black Asian woman who's directed a film that will be shown on BBC television on Christmas Day, was in the studio.

Until the last minute, however, no-one was able to tell us who the fourth member of our panel would be. When I saw four enormous men with shoulders like cornflake packets arrive I realised something was afoot. I'd only ever seen men that shape before when a Cabinet Minister appeared on the 'Today' programme on a morning when I was giving a 'Thought for the Day'. I remember once seeing Chancellor of the Exchequer Kenneth Clarke with his bodyguard and having to think twice about which one of them looked more like a prop forward! But this morning it was four such gigantic men, not just one. The explanation was simple. The man they were guarding was none other than Salman Rushdie, author of 'Midnight's Children' and the notorious 'Satanic Verses'. He's just been declared the Best Booker Prize Winner in the last twenty-five years. I've read all his stuff avidly and it was really very intriguing to sit next to him for our discussion.

And what a discussion it was. Apart from my offerings on the subject of Science and Religion, Salman Rushdie spoke about the nature of human identity in a post-colonial, cross-cultural world, and Susan Greenfield explored the nature of consciousness. At one time she talked about how excited she was when, in her anatomy class, she'd first held a human brain in her hands. She said it was like holding an oily sandwich in her fist! None of us thought our coffee tasted any the better for being face to face with that kind of comparison!

I was thrilled to be involved in a programme where we could discuss religious belief, spirituality, post-modern culture, art and literature, and the meaning of life in such an open way. It all took place under the astute chairmanship of Melvyn Bragg.

Forgive me for rambling on like this. I really am so excited that I must get it all out of my system somehow. Well, only a week now before we go to Haiti. This Presidential Year is filled with one excitement after another. See you for your birthday.

26th December 1994

Dear Tim

I'm sitting down on Boxing Day to write this to you. I'm so
full of mixed and unruly feelings. This is the first Christmas
where we haven't all been together. I'm really delighted that you
and Jo could spend the day with her parents. My heart and mind
are in agreement on that point. But I just couldn't get you out of
my head yesterday. I kept expecting to find (or hear) you when I
went into a different room or walked past your bedroom door. I
guess what I'm saying is that I missed you terribly.

I know you've been buying the 'Times' in the hope of
catching sight of my Christmas sermon. Indeed, I was asked to
supply a copy of it to the Religious Affairs correspondent post
haste and by fax. But alas! the digest of all the sermons preached
over Christmas doesn't include a word from me. The Pope, the
Archbishops, the Cardinal and Donald English are all liberally
quoted. But my little twopenny thriller didn't make the charts
this year. So you've contributed to Rupert Murdoch's profits for
nothing. You can go back to the 'Guardian' now.

Since you so wanted to see your dad's sermon in print,
perhaps you won't mind if I give you the gist of it! I explored a
deep irony at the heart of the Christmas story. Caesar Augustus
put out his famous decree and all the world jumped to. For
Augustus was a mighty, powerful man and the Roman empire,
under his leadership, reached the zenith of its power and
splendour. It's said of him that he found Rome brick and left it
marble. When he died, he was made a god and took his place in
the pantheon of gods worshipped by the Romans. The irony I
wanted to analyse is that this man, so almighty in every
conventional sense, is now largely forgotten. Meanwhile, the
little baby born to ordinary parents in unglamorous Judea is still
remembered and indeed still inspires adoration across the world.
I then went on to ask questions about the real nature of abiding
power and wondered whether we were right to look to

81

governments, armies, or big business to furnish us with any useful understanding of power in a lasting sense.

I ended my sermon with these words: 'The man who makes himself god disappears to the margins of history; his empire crumbles; his fame diminishes; he sinks into oblivion. Gone, gone forever. But the God who became man, who emptied himself of glory and took the form of a slave, is still honoured across time and space. It's at the name of Jesus (not Augustus) that knees bow and people by the million still confess that he is Lord of all. *So come, let us adore him, Christ the Lord.'*

Well, well, what a letter to write to my firstborn son on St Stephen's Day! Thanks for reading this, it's helped me cope with the conflicting emotions triggered off by your absence yesterday. Now for Haiti, we leave the day after tomorrow.

Love to Jo and her parents. Cheers.

3rd January 1995

My dear Jon

Hear we are in Haiti making a very quick but meaningful visit during the New Year period. This is the time when Haiti celebrates the Anniversary of its Independence and memories go back to that day in 1804 when people who had been slaves declared their liberty. This year, as every year since then, the people of Haiti have eaten their pumpkin soup. How I've enjoyed it – rich yellow, heavily spiced and known to everybody as *soupe libeté* (liberty soup).

My thoughts are full of you at this time. Mum and I stood this morning outside the Canapé Vert Hospital and remembered how, exactly twenty-one years ago, our little Jonathan Andrew was born there weighing 8lbs 12ozs and already smiling all over his face. We aren't very pleased that we've had to be away from you at this birthday time, but at least we've been thinking of you very deeply.

Haiti is on the move again. After the sanctions and the enforced inactivity and the years of crushing tyranny, there is space to explore new possibilities. And that space has been given, of course, by the American troops who are here in such great numbers. At the airport you see lines and lines of military helicopters, a tented village, serried ranks of heavily armed tanks and troop-carrying vehicles of all shapes and descriptions. You also see lots and lots of unrolled barbed-wire surrounding key installations where security is still very tight. It'll be nice when all this paraphernalia has gone and Haitians can take charge of their own affairs again. That's not likely to be the case for a few months yet, however.

Yesterday we met President Aristide in his private residence at Tabarre. Although it's spick and span and brand new, it's a relatively modest dwelling and it was lovely to be there. The President was making his 'State of the Nation' televised broadcast and, with a couple of dozen others, Mum and I and Ruth were able to be present and see him make the broadcast. When he'd finished, there was a short reception and some good eats and drinks for all of us.

He spent a great deal of time with the Griffiths Family, giving Mum and Ruth a big hug and a kiss, and embracing me like an old friend. He even asked me about you, remembering the time that you and he had met in August 1992 in the VIP lounge at Heathrow airport. He spoke to me about his plans for Haiti and his feelings too. He even leaned forward and whispered in my ear the names of some people whom he intends to bring into government as soon as possible. These (including Rosny Desroches) are friends of mine who've tended to be in the opposite camp from his. It's obvious he wants to bring a note of reconciliation and national unity into the running of public affairs.

The streets of Port au Prince are clean and tidy. The streetside markets are colourful and busy. Crowds and crowds of people are moving in all directions going about their daily occupations. The schools are open and transport is running. In all these ways, the contrast with my visit of just over a year ago is startling. There are other aspects, however, which leave much to be desired. Behind the street traders a significant number of shops remain empty. The owners have either fled or closed in despair after so many months of economic inactivity. And Haiti's elite continues to harbour feelings of sheer hatred and hostility towards the President and his government.

There's a lot of healing still to do. Against that, however, two of the staunchest of Aristide's foes have been making private calls to the home of the President's Chief of Staff. They're trying to patch up a deal. I only learned this accidentally and it's a little hard to square these visits with some of the things that these same people have told me face to face. But I suppose, in its way, it's encouraging that efforts at bridge-building are being made behind the scenes.

Well, I mustn't go on for much longer. I've had rare opportunities to stand publicly in an attitude of solidarity with the Haitian people at this critical juncture in their history. I preached at the Watchnight Service, led an impressively grand congregation in the renewal of their Covenant, and greeted the President of Haiti himself – all on the occasion of the celebrations of Haiti's Independence. I don't think I could have used the few days I've been here much more fruitfully than that. The President's prayer is also mine, that reconciliation and justice shall be the main ingredients in a peace which we all hope the Haitian people will enjoy long into the future.

This comes with lots of birthday love from your daddy.

Dear Mum

I'm sure you will be relieved to know that Margaret and Ruth have just arrived home from Haiti. I wasn't able to meet them at the airport because I was completing my District Visit to Birmingham. But now I'm home and we've all joined up again and there is great joy in the Griffiths' abode. They seem to have thoroughly enjoyed their extra few days in Haiti and, no doubt, I'll hear all about it over the days that follow.

I'm writing because I thought you'd be thrilled to see the little essay that Ruth has written following her return. It's so full of real feeling and insight that I wanted to share it with you at once.

You cannot know what to expect in Haiti. Any news coverage has simply not done the country justice. I was brought up in Haiti and thought I would still be intact at the end of the trip. 'Oh,' I thought, 'I shall see great poverty.' My naive and rather blasé approach to the country's problems shame me now, having seen what I have seen, and it will take a long time for the wounds to heal in me.

Poverty is a word that we use without understanding it. How can we comprehend what is so far from our experience? In Port-au-Prince, Haiti's hopelessly crowded capital, the slums are one of the most distressing things I have ever seen. Families live thirty to a room; there are a hundred families to one revolting toilet; AIDS, syphilis and tuberculosis are rife. These people have nothing, but in spite of the crippling *coup d'état*, of bloody fighting and political upheaval, they have not lost their spirit. Begging constantly, persistently asking only for a dollar, if refused they smile, laugh, and greet you in a friendly manner nevertheless.

Justice is being carried out by the people in the streets; the new American justice is not enough. Early one morning, driving through the city, we saw a man lying on the ground, stoned to death, with the pig he had stolen on top of him. A crowd was circling him warily. He had been a member of the Tontons Macoute, the feared secret police. The American soldiers would have released him from prison a few days later. The Haitians were not prepared to accept that. One night, outside our hotel, a guard was killed after an argument. Haiti still has not settled down. Feeling runs high.

But there is hope; in the streets themselves, now cleared of the rubbish which used to cover them; in the sight of men filling in the holes in the roads; in the children's homes and schools run by the Salvation Army which can be found deep within the slums of the city. But most of all it can be found in the faces of the Haitians themselves who never give up, smiling through their pain and misery. After the oppressive years of the Duvaliers, the terror of the three year *coup d'état* and the reign of the Army, the newly re-instated president, Jean-Bertrand Aristide, gives faith to his people.

Not popular with the rich of the country because of their mistrust and suspicion, Aristide is a hero to the real people. 'Viv Titid' and 'Titid is the best' are emblazoned on walls everywhere. Prophet-turned-politician, recently returned from exile after the deposal of army leader Raoul Cedras to exile in Panama, Aristide brings to politics the ideas he prayed for earlier in his life as a priest. Criticised for not having done anything since his return, a speech for Haiti's New Year Independence Day outlined the truth. This calm, elegant man exposed in the most beautiful Creole his plans for rebuilding his tragic country.

Also unpopular with the USA, one of the conditions attached to Aristide's return was that he could not be re-elected when his mandate expires next year. Despite the Americans' ostensibly channelling aid into Haiti, it is still not reaching the necessary places and will leave the country with millions of dollars worth of debt. It is difficult to imagine how Haiti can ever be put back on its feet with such responsibilities lying over it. Nevertheless, the American presence in the country, whilst appearing to be embarrassingly necessary, is having a great effect in stabilising Haiti. It would be a great blow to Haiti's security, with its army now being so drastically reduced, if the troops were withdrawn. It is very sad, however, to see such young and confused American soldiers in huge tanks watching over a people so trusting and cheerful.

Haiti is starting to change now. No longer can you see people of the slums so hungry that they bake mud into a pie and eat it, something they were reduced to when sanctions were at their tightest. New Year's Eve this year was a far cry from last year with people filling the streets and rejoicing on their national day, the 191st Anniversary of Haiti's Independence. Last year nobody came out at night; everyone was afraid to make merry. The hustle and bustle of market life has returned to the formerly empty streets. There's a long way to go yet but the people are eager to persevere in pursuit of 'dwa, ewa, jistis, rekonsiliasyon' (rights, the rule of law, justice and reconciliation). In spite of their horrendous poverty, if anyone can come out of such a situation smiling and with hope for the future, I think the Haitian people can.

Well, that's your granddaughter for you. I'm proud of her. I must leave you now, but love and kisses from us all.

Dear Kath

I'm just writing to tell you about the marvellous Civic Lunch that was given in my honour by the Lord Mayor and Lady Mayoress of Stoke-on-Trent. Margaret and I, together with Brian and Jennifer Powley, turned up on a ghastly day, a mixture of grey clouds and a furious wind punctuated with liberal doses of unexpected rain, at the Lord Mayor's Parlour in Stoke Town Hall. Awaiting us there, faces wreathed in the most enormous and generous beams of pleasure, were Richard and Laila Leigh, the current holders of the mayoral office.

We had coffee and then were shown the treasures of the City of Stoke-on-Trent. I'd expected these treasures to be made of the finest bone china and some of them were, but most were of solid silver or gold. They all spoke of the contribution of the six towns that were federated to become the city of Stoke-on-Trent in 1910 to the Industrial Revolution that swept Britain from the late 18th century onwards. Methodism, of course, played a full part in this development. Richard Leigh, in a speech he made a little later, quoted the historian who said that Britain was saved from a revolution like the one that afflicted France predominantly through the work and witness of John Wesley.

After this tête-à-tête, the Chef de Protocol (a splendid young woman who was herself, I think, a Methodist) ushered us gently out of the Parlour and, after a quick glance at the Council Chamber, we were taken to form a reception line outside the Jubilee Hall where the Civic Lunch was to take place. There we met the 70 or so guests who'd been invited. A number were, naturally, Methodists from across the Chester and Stoke-on-Trent District. Others were from Stoke-on-Trent's civic and political life including the leaders of the majority Labour group and also of the Conservative opposition. And then, finally, there were leaders of other Christian denominations – an archdeacon and a bishop from the Anglican Church, a dynamic couple of captains (man and wife) from the Salvation Army and a Roman Catholic canon.

The setting for our lunch was simply splendid. It was a formal occasion and the crockery was of the finest kind, fully fitting for Stoke-on-Trent, of course. After a sumptuous meal there were some simple speeches. Richard Leigh made a touching little oration in which he was fulsome in his welcome and which highlighted some of the major features of Stoke-on-Trent's current life. He referred to the £29 million that the city was currently expecting to help the redevelopment of Cosgrove, a rather bedraggled and deprived part of the city. He also spoke of substantial help from a larger budget which, like the £29 million, would come from the European Union's Regional Redevelopment Budget.

As I heard these details, I immediately saw an aspect of the debate about Europe that is not highlighted often enough in our press. The papers are full at the moment of worries about what'll happen when Spanish fishermen are allowed into the 'Irish box' with the consequent reduction of the British fishing fleet that will become necessary. We're always hearing these days of John Major's deferral to the Eurosceptics within his own party who, by keeping alive a picture of Europe as some kind of a many-headed monster, succeed in ensuring that our response to Europe is less than whole hearted. The fact is that, usually in non-Tory-voting areas, we are benefiting hugely from the redistribution of resources through the Brussels bureaucracy. Social development of areas that have experienced industrial decline is very considerable thanks to Europe.

Surely there is no future for these islands out of Europe. The neurotic way in which we cling to an image of former glory and a mythology of independence simply flies in the face of the facts. It so happens that Jacques Delors has just retired from being the chief European Commissioner. During his time in office he's been lambasted by the British Press and, of course, by a foghorn-mouthed Margaret Thatcher too. The fact is that, across Europe, Jacques Delors has been lauded as the most successful holder of

22 SUN. 3 aft. Epiphany.

<u>Chester & Stoke on Trent Dist.</u>

10.30 Trinity · Leek Partners in Learning
The challenge of following Jesus.

3.00 Englesea Brook lecture
'Christianity & Politics'

6.30 St George's Anglican united Service
Koinonia
Eph. 2 : 11 - 22 .

23 MON.

10.00 Nantwich - meeting with Mins etc.,

2.00 St. Margaret Ward RC School
6th Form Forum Stoke

24 TUES. ☾ 4.58 am

9.00 St. Marg . Ward RC Sch .
Xn Unity Assembly
Train Stoke
12 mins past hr — 1hr 50 mins to Euston

Car Log or Weekly Cash Account.

9 Kath
Conversion of St. Paul.   WED. **25**
9.00/9.30 Leprosy Mission - Photo
Chaplains Conference ↗ Car,
1.00 Lunch Bagshot Park
2.15 Bible. Study   Turning to
7.30 Dinner   the living God.
Soul & Peter

7.45 Communion   THURS. **26**

Luke 4 : 16-30.

Padd **BRISTOL DISTRICT** ↑
Bristol (TM)
18.45 — 20.25

9.00 Wesley College Contextual **27**
Theology in
11.30 Leyhill Prison the Inner City.

7.30 Bethesda, Cheltenham
rededication

Romans 12 : 6-11 , r. 7.46: s. 4.42   SAT **28**
8.45 Kingswood Sch. Bath
with hope in our
heart
2.30 Beechen Cliff, Bath - Consultation
with Councillors, etc

that office since it was created. Indeed, when I visited the institution of the European Union in November, a pretty neutral source told me that most people in Brussels believed that Jacques Delors could 'walk on water', so ably did he perform his work. We've missed out on a great deal by caricaturing him in the way that we have.

Back to Stoke-on-Trent! In my speech I simply paid tribute to the culture of the city which, of course, I've had occasion to enjoy for the 30 years I've been coming here since meeting Margaret in the early 1960's. I spoke of 'The Sentinel' (the local newspaper), the history of Methodism, the novels of Arnold Bennett, G M Trevelyan's 'Social History of England' and the magnificent pioneering and innovative work of Peter Cheeseman, the resident playwright and director of the wonderful Victoria Theatre. He, as much as anyone, has explored with gentle irony and the fondest affection the various aspects of Stoke-on-Trent's social and cultural history.

When the speeches were over, the Lord Mayor presented me with a marvellous Spode plate featuring the Stoke-on-Trent coat of arms with the insignia of the six federating towns surrounding it. It will occupy a place of honour in our house as soon as we get home in a few days' time.

The whole occasion was truly remarkable. For example, I thought it intriguing that a bishop of the Church of England should be asked to offer a vote of thanks both to the city and to myself. The Rev Michael Joynt-Scott, Bishop of Stafford, did this very graciously. But my abiding memory will be of the Leighs, Richard and Laila. Richard is a Circuit Steward and has been for many years. He's been active in the public life of Stoke-on-Trent for a long time and Laila has been a Local Preacher for 44 years. When the Conference last came to Stoke-on-Trent (to Burslem in 1986) Richard was in charge of the money and Laila in charge of the catering. Richard bought real china plates for the Conference meals. This seemed to be a foolhardy venture; plastic plates could have been used after all. But Richard had other things in mind. Towards the end of the Conference he announced that the plates were for sale. People queued to buy them and, as far as I know, the Stoke-on-Trent Conference was the only one ever to show a profit at the end of the day. But as I think of the Leighs, I think of that faithful commitment of so many Methodist people that I'm meeting this year across the land, loyally serving their chapel and circuit but also their community and society at large. They embody and personify the ministry of the whole people of God. It is through people like the Leighs that, because Christian conviction simply has to be translated into social action, our society might become a better place for people to live in. I salute them warmly and cherish the memory I have of them.

Sorry to have gone on at such great length. This was a smashing day. I will always remember it. See you soon.

28th January 1995

Dear Tim

I've just returned from 24 hours spent in the company of our Forces' Chaplains. They've been having a meeting in Bagshot Park down in leafy Surrey. The house and estate once belonged to the Duke of Connaught, one of the children of Queen Victoria. Its grounds are still very beautiful and there are groves (that is the only word I can think of for them) of rhododendron bushes stretching in all directions. The house itself is very grand, speaking the language of British Imperialism at the very height of its glory. The chapel wing has been completely lined in intricately carved sandalwood. This was done by Indian craftsmen brought over by Rudyard Kipling's father when the house was being built. Kipling was head of an art college in Bangalore and he brought the craftsmen all the way from India to Bagshot. They camped in tents on one of the lawns whilst they did the work inside the house.

Kipling, of course, was married to Alice McDonald, one of those four incredible sisters who all managed to marry important people (Alfred Baldwin, Edward Poynter and Edward Burne-Jones). A brother, Frederick McDonald, became President of the Conference in 1896 and all the McDonalds were descended from a father and a grandfather who were themselves Methodist ministers. So I felt at home in that part of the Duke of Connaught's house.

I was given the Chaplain General's suite! A very large sitting-room with military pictures on all the walls and antique pieces of furniture scattered around made me feel very grand. The view from the window looked over the ornamental pool and garden. I was told when registering for the Conference that I was always to remember that I was Napkin Number 1. In a rank conscious outfit like the Army such things seem to matter a great deal.

I did enjoy meeting the chaplains. I explored with them the nature of their work now that armies no longer seem to exist to fight (or win) wars but rather to make (or keep) peace. I wondered how the soldier on the ground had assimilated this relatively new understanding of the military role. The chaplains helped me to see that as long as the superior officers know what they are doing the soldier on the ground has no problem. But there's undoubtedly a big debate going on about how to draw up lines of responsibility and clear operating instructions in the new post Cold War era.

The chaplains told me about the pastoral work they do and how everything is essentially ecumenical. I told them that I had few natural or instinctive sympathies for the military but how, nevertheless, I cherished the work our chaplains do in looking after the pastoral needs of so many thousands of young people living in such difficult circumstances. They very often feel unwanted on the fringes of our Church. I'm clear, however, that chaplaincy to our Forces is an invaluable aspect of our mission to the world.

You'd have loved the dinner. It was rather formal and there was plenty of wine and good food. Napkin Number 1 sat at the centre of the top table next to the Deputy Chaplain General of the Army and various senior bods from the Airforce and the Navy. We sent the port round to the left when the meal was concluded and, after a couple of toasts, I rose to make a speech on behalf of the guests. It was rather like that time when I spoke at the rugby club dinner. Do you remember? People had drunk a lot and spirits were high but by telling a few funny stories, none of them dirty, and poking gentle fun at one or two of the prominent people present, I was able to win their attention and make one or two serious points.

I've thoroughly enjoyed my time with the military. Next week I spend a day with the RAF on location at Lyneham, Wiltshire. I'll write to you after that experience, which includes flying in a Hercules. This comes with all your dad's love.

Dear Tim

Last week I wrote to tell you I was visiting RAF Lyneham, the centre of the RAF's Transport Command. It was a super visit; the full works were laid on for me and the small party that accompanied me. We had an introductory lecture by the Wing Commander who runs the place and inspected the Chaplaincy Centre, the control tower and the recreational facilities. But, without any doubt, the highlight (in every sense of the word) was our two hour sortie in a Hercules transport plane.

The day was perfect. After lashings of rain through the previous three days, this particular afternoon turned out to be ideal. We got into our flying gear and boarded our planes. There were three in our little convoy and the whole sortie was nicknamed 'Operation Dogfish'. I was in the last of the three planes and we flew at a mere 250 feet above sea level. This was an exercise tour and the height we flew at was intended both to defeat the radar of any potential enemy and also to fly underneath any bad weather. We flew west to Exeter and then to Plymouth turning right over Dartmoor before beginning our return trip which brought us across the Quantocks and Bridgewater, Glastonbury and Wells.

In the course of that particular stretch of our flight we made a simulated touch-down on a disused Air Force base. Then we crossed Salisbury Plain. We were carrying a payload of about six large bales. The back of the aeroplane was lowered and we all stood behind the bales ready to push them out. We were rehearsing skills that the Air Force needs to employ on humanitarian sorties in places like Bosnia and Somalia. We were all strapped to a wire hawser that ran the length of the interior of the plane and we took great delight in seeing these packages disappear beneath our feet before parachutes fluttered into life to slow down their descent to the plain below. It was all very exhilarating and gave me an insight into the way in which some tricky operations are undertaken around the world.

A little side-line from all this was the military language that we employed. I heard 'ten-four' over my head phones as well as 'Roger' and, of course, 'Roger and out'! Lowering the landing gear was called 'dangling the Dunlops'. I guess a theologian shouldn't be surprised at other disciplines having a language all of their own!

We had dinner in the Officers' Mess later that evening and were able to talk about the pastoral needs of serving members of the Armed Forces and the sort of work our Chaplains do. They tend to be the forgotten ministries of our Church. Very often, in being sceptical and dismissive of military matters, we can very easily marginalise those who are undertaking some pretty important front-line work with significant numbers of people under stress.

Despite my forebodings I've enjoyed these two contacts with the military. And I've enjoyed writing to tell you all about them. Take care.

5 SUN. *5 aft. Eiphany.*

Orford & Leics District

10·30 Sandy Lane - Melton Mowbray
    All age worship.

4·00 St. Andrew's, Leicester - LP's
    Jim Drake : 100 years old
                70 years as LP.
6·30   "   "
    Mt. 8:1-17.

6 MON.

10·30 St Andrew's, Northampton-
            meeting Mins, etc.,
↓ Train Northants 14·38 - Euston 15·53

7 TUES.   D 12.54 pm

10·00 L·N·W - Min Synod - Luton
                    (Mark)

8·00 Annual Dinner Royal Inst
        Chartered Surveyors - Grosvenor
                        Park Hotel

Car Log or Weekly Cash Account.

9 Keith.   WED.   **8**

10·00 Martin Drewry

11·30 George Lovell

5·00-6·30 Launch 'Gwmg news S.A. Hope'
              HofC.

Taxi PLYMOUTH & EXETER.   THURS.   **9**
6.50 Padd 7·40 am — Exeter 10·16

    1·30 Edgehill College
Heb:2 10-18
                        Gospel in Cent'y
John 1:1-5 +10-14 7·30 Ilfracombe - Rally Society.

10·00 Devonport Dockyard   FRI.   **10**
12·15 Council House, Plymouth
    Luncheon with Lord Mayor   "
3·00 West Country TV. J.
5·30 Tea Plymouth Mission Staff
7·30 Pennycross - Circuit Rally
       Mt 8:1-17   r. 7.23: s. 5.08   SAT.   **11**

2·00 St Peter + St Paul, S. Petherton
                      Dr Cole Connections
3·00 Coke Memorial MC. Holmess
                          in Methodism

9th February 1995

Dear Jon

I've had a most interesting experience this week and I wish you'd been with me to share it. I've just attended a dinner at the Grosvenor House Hotel in Park Lane. It was the Annual Dinner of the Royal Institution of Chartered Surveyors. I was the personal guest of this year's President, a man named Roy Swanston.

It was a cold evening and I'd wondered how to get to Park Lane. Then I remembered the dear old 82 bus! Since all the guests were in formal dress and arriving by taxi or chauffeur-driven limousines, I suppose I must have been one of the very few who arrived by London omnibus. In fact, the bus goes from the end of our road to the front door of the hotel. A taxi service for the price of a bus ticket.

I wore my fifty dollar tuxedo bought in Boston last year. It looked as grand as anybody else's, I must say. The dining room was awesome; a shimmering impression of white and gold shot through with the twinkling lights of chandeliers struck me as I entered it. Beneath and within these splendid illuminations were the five hundred or so who'd come to dine. I was on the top table and asked to say grace. This I did with some relish, asking God to bless the food that was before us, the gifts of mind and character which we enjoyed, and all the resources of the earth. I then sat down to eat. And what a meal it was!

We had a mousse of salmon trout with a saffron sauce, followed by a pink champagne sorbet, climaxed by breast of duck garnished with chestnuts, mushrooms and baby onions. It was downhill all the way after that. I suppose I'm really writing to you because, apart from the splendour of the occasion, the wines were so good. We had a 1992 Chateau de Sancerre to start with – dry and yet fruity, chilled as the occasion required. This was followed by a magnificent Sylvain Fessy which, although a mere stripling from the 1993 vintage, was full-bodied and wonderful. I'm glad it's not Lent yet.

There was an extraordinary happening during the after-dinner speeches. The guest of honour was John Selwyn Gummer, the Minister for the Environment. I've found myself disagreeing with Mr Gummer on so many things in the past that I was astounded (and indeed reassured) to discover an issue on which I agreed with him. He was expressing his displeasure with the way in which members of the Institute of Chartered Surveyors had collaborated with others on all those futile schemes that result in the building of shopping malls on the edges of our cities and towns. Mr Gummer declared himself to be a keen supporter of town and city centres and intended, so he said, to apply more draconian measures to prevent people from destroying them. He was actually barracked by many of those present at the dinner. But he didn't flinch, rather he used the microphone to good effect and assured any recalcitrant surveyors that he intended to take them on and to see that they didn't do much more damage. For just a moment I thought we were outside the hotel, across Park Lane in Speakers' Corner on a Sunday afternoon. But dinner-jacketed seriousness soon returned and the meal proceeded.

I found myself sitting in an interesting place, surrounded by members of a variety of quangos. For example, on my right was the Chairman of the Institute of Arbitrators. On my left was the man who'd been Chairman of the Board for New Towns, a job he'd held for the previous 13 years. I asked him how he'd come to hold such an interesting position. Now I'm certain that I heard him aright (but I must just give him the benefit of a small element of doubt). He'd been a business man, he said, and was drawing to the end of his career. He met a senior Cabinet Minister informally (I'm sure he said it was in a public convenience). The Minister said to my companion, 'I think I've got just the job for you, old boy,' and then he proceeded to offer him the chairmanship of the quango. An interesting way to find people for these top jobs, don't you think? All very odd.

I was very touched during the speech of Roy Swanston, the President of the RICS, when he thanked me personally for being present. (My neighbour from the Institute of Arbitrators wrote a couple of days after this occasion to invite me to attend his dinner which takes place in May. Unfortunately, I can't.) He told all these important people how important his Church was for him and what an affirmation of him in this year of office my presence was. No more, no less. But it struck home with everyone and I consider it to have been an act of witness on his part. That moment alone made it worth my while being there. Here was all our thinking about 'the ministry of the whole people of God' in action.

Well, that's it. Keep smiling and don't work too hard. Love and all my best wishes.

Dear Margaret

This seems to be a particularly clogged up part of the year. It's nearly a week since I last saw you and I seem to be parcelled up and sent around various homes and lodging houses with increasing frequency. The strangest thing of all in recent times has been the fact that I even spent my birthday away from home and, of all places, in a bed and breakfast house.

I'd ended up in the B&B after a day spent at Bethany, the splendid AIDS/HIV respite home in Bodmin. I've been associated with the place almost since the beginning but have had only rare opportunities to visit it. It was grand to see Brendan Bowe carrying through the policy of giving people (so often young people) who are terminally ill opportunities to enjoy real peace and a sense of their dignity in these crucial last days and weeks of their lives. I met two residents whom I'd met on my previous visit. One was a gardener who'd landscaped many of the gardens of stately homes in the south of England. He'd also designed and set up the magnificent gardens that surround Bethany. He was there, and he knows there isn't much longer. But he's living one day at a time and it was an inspiration to see him.

I sat at the dinner table in Bethany with half a dozen others. One of them knew that he had only a few fleeting weeks left to live. He'd been that day to Tintagel and he was worn out with the effort. When we'd finished the meal, Brendan Bowe announced that it was my birthday and there was a loud cheer from the fifteen or so people who were sharing the evening meal. Then they broke into 'Happy Birthday to you' and came and slapped me on the back and wished me many happy returns. I was touched, of course, by their friendliness, but also by the fact that some of them will not be alive at my next birthday. So their wish that I might see many other birthdays came as an even greater blessing than it would usually. I was deeply moved.

After coming back from Cornwall I slid into the residential meeting of the Methodist Council. I haven't had time to talk to you about it. Many aspects of it were good, strong and constructive. And I certainly feel it's been a privilege for me to be the first President to chair it. I have to admit, however, that there are also disappointments.

The Council seemed strongly against the notion of a longer term for the President of the Methodist Conference. I've had so many conversations around the Connexion over these last months, to say nothing of views freely offered by people from outside the Methodist Church, that support a longer term. And now that I've done eight months in the job, I begin to see how this extraordinary year is like one long induction course equipping me for . . . what? Of course, as ex-President there'll be much I can do to capitalise on the experience I've gained this year. But a lot of it will also be wasted to the Church. The Council also decided to dispense with the Prayer Card, that listing of Presidential and Vice-Presidential duties which allows our Methodist people to support us in their prayers. It seems that sixty thousand have been ordered this year. But the Council was persuaded that, because some of them had not been used properly, the expenditure was wasteful. Consequently, they've abandoned the whole thing.

The poor Presidents and Vice-Presidents of the future will, I'm sure, feel the lack of it enormously. Christine and I can know that people across the country are supporting us with their prayers through this simple device. The Council seems curiously fearful of any measure which they think will confer undue power on 'leaders' or run the risk of inflating their egos. I think a longer Presidency is far from being the same as a more powerful one (in the conventional sense of the word 'powerful'). And I certainly think the Prayer Card is nothing other than a support to the holder of that office. I was deeply disappointed by the blinkered thinking of the Council on both these points.

The Council also decided that, at this time, they can't cope with changing the title 'Chairman of District' into Bishop. They wheeled out all kinds of reasons to support that view. But, at the end of the day, there is that residual fearfulness that runs right through our Methodist Church, especially by those who are supposed to be its leaders, that people are not to be trusted with power. And the title 'bishop' would, in their minds, have something to do with this dirty commodity. Once again, I felt strongly that the missionary imperative was lost to view as we followed the instinctual fears about power. So the Methodist Council was a mixture of the bright and the gloomy. I shan't be sorry to leave this level of our Church's life and return to the feet-on-the-ground life that I most cherish.

That's all for this time. Soon I shall come home and have several connected days with you. Let's go out for dinner and let's take a long walk. Let's have fun! Lots of love.

Dear Tim

I hope you don't mind me using you as part of my Lenten discipline! I've been whizzing around the country for eight months now in this Presidential Year and one experience is fading quickly into another. So I want, for the sake of my own sanity I suspect, to try and pull some of the memories together. And I thought by writing a weekly letter to you over the next six weeks I might be able to hold a number of important reflections together. I know you won't mind. You can always skip to the last paragraph if you get bored.

Earlier this week I went to Blakenhurst Prison. This is the fourth prison I've visited and there are going to be a few more yet. Blakenhurst is the second of the privatised prisons introduced by this Government. It's brand new and very well planned. This is a local jail with a total population of 650. The County and Magistrates' Courts of the West Midlands send their remand and convicted prisoners here. They stay an average of four weeks before they are dispersed to other prisons around the country.

I spoke to the Director and a number of the senior management team as well as to the chaplains. I got the sense of a prison that had begun in near total chaos but which is now pretty much delivering its goods. I'm amazed, however, how even a light and airy prison still seems such a God-forsaken hole for its inmates. I saw splendid educational facilities, Astroturf and a Gymnasium for athletic activity, and privatised cells mostly for single occupancy. But it still seemed so ugly, foul and life-denying. And such a large proportion of the inmates seemed so young, your age indeed.

The 650 inmates at Blakenhurst are part of a total prison population of fifty one thousand in British jails at the moment. This is a higher *pro rata* prison population than in just about all of our fellow European countries. And so many of the inmates could well, in my view, be offered non-custodial sentences instead of these expensive residential and gloomy prospects, which so often serve to institutionalise criminality and indeed to drive prisoners into drugs and other vices.

I've visited the Leyhill Open Prison in Gloucestershire with its 450 long-term prisoners, mainly lifers, preparing for re-integration into the community. There, I heard the Governor's bitter recriminations against the Home Secretary who had just introduced another set of knee-jerk regulations intended to tighten up on prison discipline. In particular, he'd cracked down on parole and other forms of leave. Since this is an integral part of the regime and policy of a place like Leyhill, the Home Secretary's actions were having the result of destroying prison morale.

I also visited Whitemoor, the high security jail in Cambridgeshire where terrorists and other high-risk prisoners are held. And also an old fashioned Victorian jail in Lincoln. Another aspect of life in all these places that struck me forcibly was the way Rule 43 prisoners (usually those who've committed some kind of sexual offence) have to be held separately from all the others. Although they use the same eating, recreational and educational facilities as all the other prisoners, they have to be moved around the prison in a way that gives them no contact at all. Prison culture is such that non-Rule 43 prisoners would lash out and assault the others if they came into contact with them. The logistical aspects of prison management in the light of this culture seem to me to be truly horrendous.

I'm struggling at the moment to produce the Tawney Lecture which I am to deliver for the Christian Socialist Movement in two weeks' time. The subject I've chosen is 'The Survival of Hope'. My experience of prison life through this Presidential Year has made me ask many questions about the survival of hope in our penal institutions. So many men and women are being robbed of their humanity or else forced to develop ways of coping with life that depend upon masks and deviancy and other devices of that sort. It's sometimes very hard indeed to see how our prisons can possibly rehabilitate their inmates for eventual re-entry into the community.

Before this Presidential Year, I'd only visited prisons spasmodically. This concerted round of visits, together with conversation and reflection with leading thinkers in the field, is helping me to understand this dimension of our national life with a great deal more sensitivity. I've heard prison officers speaking of inmates as if they were beasts. I've heard others going more than the second mile to see that self-awareness courses were offered diligently to the prisoners in their charge. I've heard Governors rail against the Home Secretary; and other officers lament that he isn't showing enough strength of character. I've heard prisoners talk about Bible study and prayer. And I've seen simply magnificent chaplaincy service offered in prison after prison. Very often it's the chaplaincy team that keeps a note of sanity sounding at every level of a prison's life. Thank God for our chaplains.

Well, I don't know how you've coped with this letter, my dear boy. Just think of it. Another five to come!

I hope you wore your daffodil for St David's Day. This comes with all my love.

My dear Tim

Last week it was prisons, this week it's poverty. My Lenten exploration of brokenness and despair continues. Last Saturday I attended some 'Poverty Hearings' being held at Teeside University in Middlesborough. Three hundred people were gathered and a number of them spoke. But the undoubted highlight of the afternoon were the seven testimonies given by people who were experiencing poverty in one shape or another. These seven people were not theoreticians, professional analysts, or theologians. They were simple people trying to explain to their audience what poverty meant and how they were trying to cope with it. The whole afternoon, together with a series of similar Hearings across the country, was organised by Church Action on Poverty.

One contributor named Colin gave a clear step-by-step analysis of the stages through which you go when you become unemployed. I found this to be as insightful as the similar talk given by Elizabeth Kubler-Ross when she analysed the different stages of bereavement. Colin indicated that his initial response to unemployment as an experienced tradesman was *optimism* that, at 40 years of age, he'd soon find something else. But this was soon followed by *realism* when his first attempts to find another job failed. Two hundred and fifty applications later, realism was replaced by *frustration*. At this stage he was given careers advice that he found useless. This largely amounted to being told that he needed to 'look younger' when he applied for jobs! This was followed by *anger*. By then he'd had enough of other people's 'attitudes'. He decided to take a radically different approach to the matter and enrolled for educational courses at the Open University and elsewhere. But even this got him nowhere in terms of finding a new job. And now he confesses to being consumed by *bitterness, apathy* and *despair*.

As he looks around him he sees third generation unemployment in his community and considers this to be a very dangerous phenomenon. He pointed to the South Bank housing estate (which I'd visited earlier that same day) as evidence of what happens to a community of people who have no horizons or hope. Drugs, wanton violence, total alienation and apathy are the hallmark of life on that estate. Houses have been burned out, are boarded up and people live in fear of the next incident.

Others spoke of the clear link between unemployment and poverty. One of the contributors named Shaun had written a poem. 'What's it all for?' he shouted, 'The pain of dying slowly won't go away.' Throughout the poem phrases like 'out of control', 'self-destruct button', 'I'm slipping into despair' kept reappearing. And this was very much the tone of others who spoke. Linda was a single parent with two children. She felt herself constantly judged by others to be a wicked person. Sometimes she found herself secretly agreeing with such judgements. She remembered the recent statement from a Government Housing Document that suggested that 'single parents only get pregnant to get a roof over their heads'. Yet she was on her own because the fathers of her two children refused to take any responsibility and had abandoned the home. The DSS wouldn't let her do voluntary work, and she had ended up eking out her benefits by doing sweated labour as a cleaner for £15 a week. She was often in despair. Tears were her daily lot. Bewilderment and pain racked her being. It was clear from this and much else that the whole audience felt the need to make the reality of poverty clear to those who believed it did not exist.

Then I spoke to offer 'theological reflection' on all that we'd heard. I quoted the Opposition motion that had been before the House of Commons a few weeks ago when they debated poverty and unemployment and the Rowntree Report (which had indicated a widening gap between the richest and poorest members of our society). The motion began 'that this House condemns the damage done to the country's social fabric and economy by the rapid growth of poverty in the United Kingdom's society; deplores Government policies which have failed the long-term unemployed . . .' I then quoted the Government amendment which was ultimately carried and whose tone and temper were so radically different from the original motion. This is how it went. 'That this House welcomes the fact that the vast majority of people are significantly better-off today than in 1979 . . . approves the Government's policy of ensuring that Social Security spending does not outstrip the nation's ability to pay . . . applauds the fact that the Government has channelled an extra billion pounds a year to low income families . . . welcomes the high priority accorded by the Government to education and training . . .'

When I read out this later motion the whole audience gasped in disbelief. The only theological reflection I felt able to offer was the often repeated word of Jesus in the New Testament when he urged those who have ears to hear and those who have eyes to see what's happening around them. How can people look at a society like ours in which poverty so manifestly exists without apparently recognising what they see; or hear the cries of the poor, which reach to heaven itself, without being stirred into a caring response? It's a complete mystery to me.

And thus the second Lenten epistle draweth to its end. All my love.

My dear Tim

I continue my series of meditative Lenten letters about some of the gloomier aspects of British society as I'm meeting them this year as President of Conference. You've been so kind to read my previous offerings and to encourage me to continue. It's part of my seasonal discipline, to walk the way of (other people's) suffering as we approach the season where the cross figures centrally in our devotions before we finally reach the more positive news of Easter Sunday.

This week it's the homeless that I'm worried about. Last week I spoke to some 600 teenagers all gathered for the 50th Anniversary celebrations of MAYC. You know better than most that I'm not really a 'young persons' minister'. I can't really claim to have much contact with your culture or to understand very deeply what issues seem to matter most to you. But I was most moved by what I saw on that occasion. MAYC is concentrating this year, its Jubilee, on the question of homelessness and is urging young people across the land to go into their local communities to find out just what's going on. And they're doing this with great energy and zeal. I take my hat off to them.

It's only a couple of weeks since I went to the Piccadilly Advice Centre in Shaftesbury Avenue. Shelter, who've been supplying me with briefing materials for all my District Visits this year, have just taken over this Centre's running. What a story they have to tell! In the course of one year they've received some 27,841 enquiries. More than half of those have been by telephone but 12,000 people have physically presented themselves at the counter. They've been desperate for somewhere to stay. Can a night shelter place be found for them? Is there somewhere to go during a cold weather spell? Are there any hostels available? And so on and so forth. There was a board in the office showing the list of night shelters and hostels contacted daily by the Piccadilly Advice Centre. It was grim to read the word FULL against every single one. That is, at three o'clock in the afternoon of a cold March day, there were no places available that night for anybody who might be desperate. The staff at the Centre were pulling their hair out with frustration and despair.

In the course of this year I've really tried hard to visit projects that are attempting to meet the needs of homeless people. Just at random, I can think of work I've become aware of in Preston, Bradford, Bourne (Lincolnshire), Norwich, Lincoln, York, Exeter, several places in London, Birmingham and Manchester. I can think of day centres, night shelters, housing associations and advice centres. I can think of schemes that meet the first aid needs of those who have nowhere to stay. And I can think of information gathering and analysis and a readiness to get stuck into the unpopular business of educating the public. And I can also think of the Churches' National Coalition on Housing, which tries to organise people to campaign on behalf of the homeless. If genteel and middle-class people can get angry on behalf of animals then they should get hopping mad at the continuing and persistent homelessness that abounds in this land.

It's curious, isn't it, that living in Margaret Thatcher's Finchley we can still see the prevalence of homelessness in a big way. My colleague Mark Booth and his friends at Ballards Lane are running a soup ministry where 150 people are fed week by week. There's a clothing store and a medical service for those in need. And similar efforts are being made at a local synagogue and also at the Bourne Methodist Church in Southgate. Who'd have thought that in this archetypal leafy suburb homelessness on that scale actually exists?

In addition, Mark has been working for some time now with another group of friends in Homeless Action Barnet, to try to get a Day Centre organised to serve the continuing needs of homeless people in the Borough. At last he seems to be in sight of finding somewhere. And, of course, my own efforts with

Andrew Redfern to try to build 23 units of accommodation for psychiatrically disturbed homeless people makes me aware of how many victims there are from the under-resourced 'Care in the Community' programme, which has pushed so many psychiatrically disturbed people on to our streets. The problems don't seem to go away and Christians cannot wash their hands of a responsibility to struggle with the victims for a more just situation to prevail.

Of course, I've told you often enough about that time in my own infancy when my father kicked my mother and her two boys out of the family home. I was too young to remember how my mother coped in detail. But I don't think I'll ever forget the feelings of being homeless, an emptiness in the pit of the stomach, a perpetual anxiety, and a restlessness that was only satisfied when finally we found somewhere to live.

So we must go on remembering that homeless people are precisely that – people. As the young people put it in a little play they did at the big service last week, the homeless are regularly sterotyped and labelled: 'Most of them are drunks', they 'might be violent', 'it's their own fault' . . . and so on and so forth. Yet in the same sketch the picture was put across of one person who was homeless because his job folded up; another whose marriage had collapsed; another who'd grown up in care. All these were perfectly 'normal' members of society who, through circumstances they couldn't control, ended up on the streets.

Well, I must leave you now. But I hope you've inherited some of my passion for the struggle against this social evil. In the Old Testament there's a word about the ultimate blessing being when you can sit outside your own house in peace, a house that's permanent with an olive tree growing in the garden and a vine producing its grapes. Why shouldn't everybody enjoy such blessings?

This comes with all your daddy's love.

My dear Tim

Here I am again, offering another line of deeply
introspective thought for this season of Lent. After the prisoners,
the poor and the homeless, this week my mind is full of a
different kind of impoverishment. I'm preoccupied just at the
moment with the nature of politics in our country and the total
alienation from the political process of such significant numbers
of our people.

As you probably know from your telephone calls to mum,
my mind has been grappling for weeks and weeks with a lecture
which I gave last Saturday in the Gothic splendour of All Saints'
Church, Margaret Street, in the West End of London. This is a
kind of Mecca for very High Anglicans and proved to be a
splendid setting for the R H Tawney Lecture which I gave for the
Christian Socialist Movement. This church, it appears, had
played a significant part in the Christian Socialist Movement
during the latter part of the 19th century.

I was stunned by the large number of people present –
hundreds, who were singing their way lustily through the hymn
'Be thou my vision' when mum and I arrived. Since I'd been
expecting a mere couple of dozen I was, to put it mildly,
overwhelmed by the multitude.

My lecture was called 'The Survival of Hope'. For me,
hope has to do with this world and necessitates a readiness on
the part of all people of good will to get involved in the task of
making it a more just and better place for others to live in. I
traced what I called 'Fallacies of Hope' which were the ruined
ideologies and the presumptuous political movements that had
promised deliverance and salvation and had been proved by
events to be bankrupt. All theories of the left and the right which
promised the inevitability of progress, a deterministic
understanding of the forward movement of history, and the

perfectibility of man were proved now to be totally unable to deliver. If that, in fact, is true then where is hope to be found?

I then began a section called 'Crossing the threshold of Hope'. For me, hope comes from the fact that one human being has the capacity to feel the pain and share the joy of another. That means that we are not locked into ourselves. The fellow-feeling and the compassion that another person's plight can engender in me is proof that we are not intended to live utterly selfish and self-seeking lives. There is a capacity for forming links with others and it's upon that realisation that all notions of community are to be built.

Then I went into my third point. This was called 'With Hope in your Hearts'. It was an extended treatment of the social teaching of the Roman Catholic Church based upon 'Centesimus Annus', a papal encyclical that highlights two important points. Firstly, solidarity – the fellow-feeling and interdependence that I hinted at in my previous paragraph. And secondly, subsidiarity – that notion, that however we are governed, we must be involved in that process in every way that's reasonable and possible. That is, we are to participate in the shaping of the events around us and the decisions that govern us.

I ended with a little bit of a tirade, I suppose. I suggested that it was a Labour government that was best placed to deliver programmes that could maximise solidarity and the principle of subsidiarity. I criticised the Conservative governments of recent years for giving undue prominence to the self, to selfishness and to individuality at the expense of community. But I also urged the Labour Party to work hard, long before a general election appears on the horizon, to have its package of 'constitutional measures' up and ready so that they could be announced in the very first Queen's Speech after they had won the next General Election. For it's in changing some of the ways in which we are governed, notably through proportional representation and increased constitutional rights for the citizens of the land, and accountable local government with appropriate powers, that the notions of solidarity and subsidiarity to which I'd referred would be delivered.

Of course, the media got hold of my criticisms of the Government. I was quoted on the radio news programmes as having slated the Tory administration and having criticised the Roman Catholic Church. How the media love to turn carefully developed arguments into headlines! The BBC reporter had turned up only 15 minutes before the end of my speech because, having had a written copy of it sent him by our Press Office, he knew 'which were the interesting bits' that he wanted to use. And they were, of course, the conflictual and critical ones. Sometimes I despair of the way journalists go about their work.

My lecture was intended to address the needs of a people who have been starved intellectually and spiritually over the last few years and have, consequently, kept their distance from the political process. Our democracy depends upon winning them back again. But they'll only be won back again when they sense that they are being heard, taken seriously and respected. I'm sure that Christians must play their part in seeking to reverse the tendencies of recent years.

I'm sure that this season of Lent, which pushes us Christians to consider the way love stands in judgement over all our struttings and frettings on the stage of life, needs us to look at the re-investing of our political life with the note of hope. I ended my lecture by twisting an old, old quotation from the 17th century so that it read as follows:

> In the year 1996/7 when all things sacred were throughout the nation either demolished or profaned, a progressive administration was formed in Westminster, whose singular praise it is to have done the best things in the worst times; and hoped them in the most calamitous.

I wonder if you've kept awake as you've struggled through this heavy letter. There'll be another one next week!

My dear Tim

Lent continues and so do my dark thoughts about the kind of world we're living in. This week I've been prompted by pictures, haunting pictures, on the television screen from Burundi. There they go again, those dishevelled lines of fragile humanity making their way to God knows where in some camp in Tanzania or Zaire, where everything already seems to be cracking under the strain.

My sense of horror is compounded by the fact that I should be there myself. Just a few days ago, I got a phone call from the WCC in Geneva asking me to head a team of Church leaders going to Burundi to show solidarity with Church leaders there at this critical time. We all remember so graphically what happened in Rwanda. This time, we want at least to be present before the most dreadful dimensions of this crisis reveal themselves. And I had to say no because of the rigidity of my Presidential diary. So the pictures sear my soul as I look at them.

As I think about all these refugees in Central Africa, I remember that they are part of the ghastly total of five million displaced people on the African continent alone. I remember well enough seeing those lorries full of Mozambican refugees making their tawdry and empty way back from years of exile in Malawi. That was nine months ago. What were they going back to? Their land has been ravished by 30 years of war, the communities they belong to exist no longer, there is no infrastructure to hold them together, and life looks bleak for years to come. And what of the people they've left behind? The people of Malawi have made way for a million refugees over the last generation. They've lost their land, and the economy of the whole region has been affected by the aid and sustenance programmes that have been mounted by the international community. And now these same lands are to be emptied. Those left behind have developed a culture of dependence upon the aid organisations and will not easily re-establish their agrarian economy. Their plight is parlous indeed.

All these sombre thoughts come on top of new insights on the matter I received recently from my visit to Geneva. Whilst there, I was told that there are more refugees and displaced people in the continent of Europe now than at any time since the Second World War. Many of these, of course, are to be found in the war-torn parts of the former Yugoslavia. Ethnic cleansing, mass rape, displacement of whole populations and religious divisions have all contributed to the chaotic fracturing of traditional societies there. And in the southern republics of the former Soviet Union, similar dreadful disruption has taken place. In the meantime, the European Union seems to be organising itself to keep the overspill from these areas of confusion at bay. Fortress Europe raises metaphorical walls at least as frightening as the real one recently destroyed in Berlin.

I visited a Detention Centre in Rochester recently with the newly appointed Bishop, Michael Nazir-Ali. It was awful to see these miserable and pitiable specimens of humanity all trussed up and ready to be veal-caged back to such hell holes as Zaire, Somalia and Sierra Leone. There'll be no nice, middle-class English matrons at the ports of exit to protest against this human cargo. If only I'd had a magic wand and could have waved it over these, the lowest forms of humanity, I'd have turned them into week-old calves and shipped them from Shoreham just to see whether there would even have been one pipsqueak voice raised in opposition to such human traffic.

And so this time, my dear Tim, it's the plight of refugees that preoccupies me. As I think of Jesus walking through the valley of the shadow of suffering and shame, reviled by the polite society of his day, spat upon and mocked, I somehow see a capacity in him to walk with these poor, broken men, women and children in the time of their greatest need. And how I wish that the followers of Jesus would carry the burdens of this displaced humanity more readily upon their shoulders, accepting a common responsibility for their lot, and working for the day when peace will reign around this beautiful world, giving hope where there is now despair, and bringing light where darkness seems currently so totally in command.

As always, this comes with your daddy's love.

Lent 6   11th April 1995

Dear Tim

We're now into the last lap before Easter. Before the
message of light and hope comes crashing in upon us, dispelling
the gloom of Passiontide, we've got to agonise our way through
the final days of Holy Week. I always find this the most
searching time of the year. Despite the fact that I've preached
and taught about it for many years now, it still proves to be a
searing encounter with deep and threatening forces, a message
which reminds me of man's capacity to show inhumanity to
other human beings.

Palm Sunday this year coincided with the 50th anniversary
of the death of Dietrich Bonhoeffer. Since very early in my life,
Bonhoeffer has been a significant figure for me. He was a
brilliant theologian, an ecumenical church leader, and a very
well-connected member of Germany's upper middle-class. He
took a very brave stance against the Nazis and, in the end,
decided to throw his lot in with a group that was plotting the
death of Hitler. He had to make the most awful choice in the
world: either to keep his hands clean and to operate solely within
the confines of the Church, or else to be prepared to collaborate
in killing Hitler and thus release many thousands of people from
the oppressive force of his jackboot. Bonhoeffer was arrested,
and finally hung at Flossenburg just a few days before the end of
the war. It was a tragic waste, of course.

But somehow it was also a poignant and deep identification
with the self-offering of Christ. Bonhoeffer's become a martyr
and an inspirational figure; his 'Letters and Papers from Prison'
are a spiritual classic of this century. And, somehow, behind him
I keep on seeing and half-hearing all those people who were the
victims of Nazism and the Gestapo. The cry of Christ, 'My God,
my God, why have you forsaken me?' seems to come from all
those camps where millions of people ended their lives so
miserably. I honour the memory and the prophetic ministry of

Dietrich Bonhoeffer and pray that I may have even a fraction of his courage and clear-sightedness.

This also happens to be the season where the anniversary of Martin Luther King's assassination falls. It's 27 years since his death. Once again, I can half see this brave Baptist pastor calling his people into non-violent protest against the racism of America. I can't forget that King was a personal friend of Willard Williams, father of my own friend Wesley Williams, a Methodist minister working in Boston, Massachussetts. And I've heard the tale from Willard's own mouth of the marches and the demonstrations, the preaching and the speeches, and the idealism which all focused in the person of Martin Luther King. He knew he was risking death. Yet he did not shrink from the challenge. Once again, the exploration of the limits of human endurance, so clearly evident in the person of Christ, has been pursued by one of his followers in our age. And behind Martin Luther King, and from somewhere in the middle distance of time, I can hear the voices of all those black people who were shipped over from Africa's shores to infamy and slavery and subjection in the 'New World'. Once again, though they sang the most magnificent spirituals, the deep and haunting note of their music is one of melancholy and despair. They were obliged to focus their hopes of justice upon some heaven rather than here on God's own earth.

Bonhoeffer and King are two of the martyrs whose anniversaries fall at this time. Oscar Romero is a third. It's 15 years since he died in El Salvador. He championed the cause of his people in the struggle against the malign forces of reaction and oppression (often funded hugely from the United States of America). And he died at his altar, in the very presence of the bread and wine, those effectual tokens of the one and only sacrifice which can take away the sin of the world. The Lamb of God is indeed a sacrificial lamb. And in every age some of his followers share in that sacrifice by making the supreme offering of their lives.

I salute the memory of Oscar Romero, Martin Luther King and Dietrich Bonhoeffer, and all those martyrs whose blood is the seed of the Church. I thank God for all the Christ-likeness that I see in their supreme offering of themselves. And I pray that succeeding generations will not only honour their memory but walk in their footsteps. The powers of evil and destruction can be challenged only when people draw deeply on the courage that God gives them to fight and resist and struggle against the de-personalising forces that stalk through the land. The cross is about nothing less than that.

Easter comes soon. Prepare for the explosion of joy. With all my love.

My dear Tim

You've borne with me so patiently as I've explored my Lenten themes. Now that's all done with and we turn over the page from the forty days of self-discipline and waiting to the great end-point of arrival. It's Easter and, once again, we try to wrap our minds around the great mystery of the Life that could not be crushed – even by Death.

I'm writing this from the Channel Islands. I'm sitting in a room in Jersey's Biarritz Hotel with stupendous views over St Brelade's Bay directly below me. Since our arrival here last Thursday, the springtime sun has shone and the whole of nature seems to proclaim the survival of hope over the dark winter forces of despair. Not only nature, with its blossom and new greens in such varied abundance, but also history shouts out the message of new life. St Brelade (from whom this part of the island takes its name) was one of a number of sixth century Celtic saints (trained at Llantwit Major!) who roved and roamed the lands bordering the Channel in ceaseless evangelical endeavour. They overcame much suffering and hunger and shipwreck. They were mighty in all that they did.

The nineteenth century added its own chapter of missionary zeal to that of the sixth. Upwards of eighty Methodist missionaries went to serve the fledgling outreach work then being undertaken in France. Twenty more went to Haiti. I just wish I could impress on the modern inhabitants of these islands just how fantastic this outburst of energy really was. Young men (sometimes married, often single) went from Jersey, Guernsey, Alderney and (yes!) Sark to serve in Haiti. Some, like Mark Baker Bird (the architect of Haitian Methodism) suffered hugely but, consenting to become more vile, stuck it out all the same. They buried their children and their wives on Haitian soil, they saw their property and possessions burned in successive revolutions, they endured earthquakes and hurricanes, they were persecuted and despised. But they kept on going all the same.

All of this speaks to me the language of unkillable life. It's in such doings and goings that I perceive the ongoing availability of all that the resurrection represents: new and resurgent life that challenges every force that seeks to diminish human hope and kill the human spirit. As I sit here in Jersey, I seem to see in nature's open volume and also in the faces of the host of surrounding witnesses the evidence of Christ's victory over death. It's a marvellous time to be alive.

Just yesterday mum and I, together with the Chairman of the Channel Islands District, were invited to call on the local Rabbi. The Jews are celebrating Passover and we attended their evening prayers. Passover is, of course, the time when Jews give thanks to God for the way he led them out of captivity in Egypt and directed them towards their promised land, a land flowing with milk and honey. The angel of death 'passed over' the children of Israel, they were spared his deprivations and they were led forth through the Red Sea into their liberation. It so happens that the very day we were with the Jewish congregation thinking these exodus thoughts, it was the fiftieth anniversary (to the day) of the liberation of Belsen. Our newspapers had been full of pictures and stories of that awful place where, on the day the British army of liberation arrived, some 35,000 bodies lay in anonymous and skeletal heaps while a further 30,000 'living dead' stared out at the soldiers who had come unawares to rescue them. The angel of death hadn't done much passing by in Belsen (or Buchenwald, or Auschwitz).

And Jews celebrating Passover, to say nothing of Christians rejoicing at *their* passover festival (that's what Easter is after all, for the angel of death has been dealt a definitive blow by the resurrection of Jesus), can hardly do so oblivious to the great sufferings that still go on in the world around us. The forces of death are still abroad in the land. Jews and Christians have special reasons to go on working for the alleviation of suffering wherever they find it. For suffering and shame, evil and death, are the very enemies that were dealt a mortal blow by the first and second exodus. Those who live as the children of the resurrection are the sworn enemies of all that drags people towards death and ignominy. That's why I've written the gloomy Lenten letters that precede this one. And that's why I want to end this set of missives with my adaptation of part of an ancient Christian hymn. I've modified it so as to include all the marginalised people I've been writing about through Lent. After all, they too have their part in that great army of people who praise God for all his love and for all his goodness.

A truly happy Easter to you and Jo,
Dad

We praise thee, O God, we acknowledge thee to be the Lord.
All the earth doth worship thee, the Father everlasting.
To thee all angels cry aloud, the heavens and all the powers therein.
To thee cherubim and seraphim continually do cry:

Holy, holy, holy, Lord God of Sabaoth;
Heaven and earth are full of the majesty of thy glory.

The glorious company of the *homeless* were made by thee;
The goodly fellowship of the *poor* are all thy sons and daughters;
To thee belong all *prisoners*, their voices reach thy throne;
Thine too are all those *alienated* and also the *oppressed*;
The vast multitudes of *refugees* have honour in thy sight;
The noble army of *martyrs* worship and praise thy holy name;
All these, the poor, the wretched of the earth, together with
The *Holy Church* throughout all the world do acknowledge thee

The Father of an infinite majesty,
Thine honourable, true and only Son,
Also the Holy Ghost, the Comforter;

For ever and ever, till time is no more; Alleluia, Amen.